DOES GOD HATE LESBIAN *Women?*

REVEREND BONNIE KELLY

B.A., McGill University, 1972
M. Div., Emmanuel College, 1980

Submitted to the Faculty of Theology Acadia Divinity
College In partial fulfillment of the requirements
for the degree of Doctor of Ministry

Acadia Divinity College
Acadia University
May Convocation 2006

Copyright © 2014, 2024 Reverend Bonnie Kelly.

All rights reserved. No part of this book may be reproduced, stored, or transmitted by any means—whether auditory, graphic, mechanical, or electronic—without written permission of both publisher and author, except in the case of brief excerpts used in critical articles and reviews. Unauthorized reproduction of any part of this work is illegal and is punishable by law.

ISBN: 979-8-89419-067-9 (sc)
ISBN: 979-8-89419-068-6 (hc)
ISBN: 979-8-89419-069-3 (e)

Because of the dynamic nature of the Internet, any web addresses or links contained in this book may have changed since publication and may no longer be valid. The views expressed in this work are solely those of the author and do not necessarily reflect the views of the publisher, and the publisher hereby disclaims any responsibility for them.

One Galleria Blvd., Suite 1900, Metairie, LA 70001
(504) 702-6708

Contents

Abstract..v
Dedication vii
Acknowledgements ix
Preface xi
Introduction xv

Chapter 1 Theological and Theoretical Framework for this Study..1
  The Biblical Basis of Pastoral Care 1
  Freedom of Conscience 5

Chapter 2 A Brief History of the Gay Liberation Movement 11

Chapter 3 Pastoral Care Issues for Lesbian Women 13
  Grief and Loss 13
  Anger..18
  The Families-of-Origin of Lesbian Women..........21
  Reaction: Lack of Hospitality....................24

Chapter 4 Finding A Place of Belonging in The Church 29

Chapter 5　　Research: The Stories 37
　　　　　　　Betty's Tape 37
　　　　　　　Pam's Tape. 44
　　　　　　　Joy's Tape 56
　　　　　　　Mary's Tape 66
　　　　　　　Jeanine's Tape. 80
　　　　　　　Elizabeth's Tape 97

Chapter 6　　Analysis of The Stories 103
　　　　　　　Analysis of Betty's Interview. .103
　　　　　　　Analysis of Pam's Interview 105
　　　　　　　Analysis of Joy's Interview 107
　　　　　　　Analysis of Mary's Interview .108
　　　　　　　Analysis of Jeanine's Interview 110
　　　　　　　Analysis of Elizabeth's Interview 114

Conclusion 117
Endnotes. 119
Appendix A: Consent Form. 123
Appendix B: Thesis Proposal and Questions for Interviews. 125
Bibliography 127

Abstract

This paper is about the pastoral care of lesbian women by the Church. The first part of the paper deals with our Biblical mandate to provide pastoral care, personal conscience, the gay liberation movement, and the experiential reality of lesbian persons.

Six lesbian women were interviewed in reference to their experience with the Church as children and then as adults as they went through a process of self-identification and the search for belonging.

An analysis of all six of the interviews was made in reference to their affiliation with the Church and as recipients of pastoral care.

The results portrayed a picture of the Church lacking in uniformity in reference to the care lesbian women are receiving from the Church. It is evident, however that the pastoral care offered to lesbian women by the Church at this point in time is in definite need of growth in understanding and conscious delivery.

Dedication

To Mary

Acknowledgements

In honour of all the wonderful teachers in my life, my parents, Roland and Mary Kelly, Kathryn Anderson, Dr. Shelley Finson, countless loving parishioners, and two wonderful secretaries: Dessie Rafue and Marilyn Roberts.

Preface

Caroll A. Wise, in his book, **The Meaning of Pastoral Care** emphasizes that pastoral care is the ministry of a person who stands in the same relationship to God as do the persons to whom they minister. There is to be a profound respect on the part of the minister for the unique journey and being of the "other."

It is my belief that as much as the Church has offered excellent pastoral care to countless varieties of people, it has not done a good job in respect to lesbian women. This sector of the population has been, for the most part, largely hidden for many reasons. One of these reasons is the perceived hostility and lack of understanding on the part of the Church. In this paper I would like to further the cause of understanding on the part of the Church and to hopefully help the Church to offer pastoral care in a more informed manner to lesbian women.

The Church has had a great deal to say about lesbian women based largely upon its various interpretations of the scriptures. In this paper, I would like to give voice to what some lesbians have to say to the Church about their lives vis-à-vis the Church. Perhaps it will be hard to listen.

In this paper, I have certain assumptions:

1. Lesbian women are loved as much by God as anyone else.
2. The pastoral care offered to them as to all people must be of the highest caliber.
3. The Church has a need to rethink its traditional assumptions about lesbian women.
4. Lesbian women are not sinners condemned by God.
5. The lesbian 'lifestyle' is not a deliberate sinful choice, but rather an expression of a natural orientation.
6. The Church must listen to lesbian women with understanding love.
7. Lesbian women have suffered deeply because of the Church.
8. The Church must repent when it grows beyond long-held beliefs; as it is led by the Holy Spirit.
9. The Church has not deliberately or knowingly neglected, denigrated, or caused lesbian women to suffer.

We have the ministry of the Church not of ourselves, in our own strength, but as followers of Jesus Christ. He is the Author and Finisher of our faith and our mandate comes from him. Jesus was very intentional about listening to others with understanding love, and reflecting deeply on what he had heard. Jesus is our model. It is one that is not complicated; but calls for tremendous focus and searching. All preconceptions must be jettisoned and truth be given space and air. We have been the "keepers of the Truth" in the Church for centuries. We have taught "the Truth."

"As God has sent me, so send I you" (John 20:21 NRSV). What Jesus expected was that the pastoral ministry be directed toward the needs of the people for equality, for dignity, and for help as dealing with the burdens of life. It is not in any way the purpose of the Church of Jesus Christ to burden people with condemnation, degradation, and lack of understanding. If the Church cannot offer proper pastoral care to lesbian women with compassion and grace, then it needs to be very clear about that. Too many lesbian women grew up in the Church believing they were loved and cherished only to experience the trauma of condemnation once their sexuality was discovered or shared with others in the faith community. We hear the words of Jesus crying from the Cross, "My God, my God why have you forsaken me?" Many lesbian women in the Church have experienced a tremendous sense of betrayal not only by God, but by their beloved Church family.

Pastoral care is about the redemption and care of persons. The Church also needs redemption in some areas of its life. I would propose the thesis that the Church needs to be redeemed from its systemic lack of understanding and compassion for lesbian women.

Introduction

When I began my Doctor of Ministry degree I was working in an Anglo-Saxon congregation as a Pastoral Minister in Northern Ontario. We were embedded in an Aboriginal context of Ojibway and Cree people who had a very different understanding of what spirituality was all about. Although I had a degree in Cultural Anthropology, there were many things I realized these people could teach me; if I had the humility to listen.

As with many cultures of the world, storytelling is used as the principle means whereby truths are communicated in the Aboriginal community. Profound respect is given when another speaks of their soul's journey. People sit in a circle, each one being accorded an equal place in the "circle of belonging". No one is to comment on the story; they are only to listen and to take learnings from it that have meaning for them. No one is silenced. No one is rushed. No one is forced to speak if they choose not to. No one is called a "sinner". No one is thrown out of the circle because of their sharing.

I left honoured to be included in the "circle of sacred storytelling" when invited. I was profoundly moved not only by the stories, but by the courage with which these people lived their lives in the face of tremendous desecration of their culture, their spirituality and their personhood.

I will be forever transformed and sensitized because I have heard these sacred stories. It was painful to pass through the terrible process of knowing that the Church I love and serve has been involved historically in a very profound and unspeakable way in the suffering and desecration of a people. This reality continues to affect their lives. As Christians, we have too often been arrogant and disrespectful and have silenced people while we foisted our theologies upon them. I am appalled and ashamed. We would not listen. We would not hear. We had all the "right" answers.

Because of this experience with the power of personal storytelling to transform and enlighten, I decided to do qualitative research in the area of narrative storytelling. I chose six lesbian women between the ages of 40-60 years of age to interview. I offered them the opportunity to share their sacred stories with the Church. I chose middle-aged lesbians for my research because they have, by this time in life, considerable life experience as well as a knowledge of what, for them, is the truth of their being. As we journey along in life our sense of self solidifies. In my research, I have attempted to honour what has been for each of these women, an excruciating, joyful, frustrating journey. They have had to peel off layers of societal overlay, as we all do, to find the sacred self. The search for self is a private matter between a person and God as they come to understand God. Protestant theology has always supported the belief in personal conscience. Most lesbian women have had others tell them who they are for centuries. It is only in our time, with the advent of the Gay Liberation Movement, that they are finding their voice in the arts and in every institution in society. They have long had the need to speak their truth to an often disparaging world. This book is but a small effort to that end.

My theology would say to me that when I do not allow another to speak their truth and honour that truth then I have dishonoured God in whose image we are all fashioned. "If one member suffers, all suffer together with it; if one member is honoured, all rejoice together with it." (1 Corinthians 12:26 NRSV).

It has been a great honour and privilege to interview six lesbian women. I approached them with the Christian mandate to live God's compassion for one another. My hope is that these stories will form the basis of a transformational encounter with the reader. The Swiss theologian, Paul Tournier has said:

> "What counts for me is encounter. Encountering other people, a particular person, an idea, nature – encountering God, who is hidden behind all these encounters."[1]

CHAPTER ONE

Theological and Theoretical Framework for this Study

The Biblical Basis of Pastoral Care

As Christians our whole hope is to embody the Christ in God's world. Our living model for the pastoral care of people is the person and work of Jesus, the Christ, as portrayed in the gospel accounts of his life and teaching. It is the calling of the Minister as well as the lay people to mediate something of the quality of being, which is found in the revelation of Christ in their ongoing living relationships. This living relationship has the hallmark of forgiveness, reconciliation, and healing. It is within this living relationship that God's Holy Spirit is at work giving the insight and power so essential for daily living.

The mandate for offering pastoral care in the form of healing the sick, raising the dead, cleansing the lepers, and casting out demons is found in Matthew 9:35-10:16: (NRSV).

> "And Jesus went about all the cities and villages, teaching in their synagogues and preaching the gospel of the kingdom, and healing every disease and every infirmity.[36] When he saw the crowds he had compassion for them, because they were harassed and helpless, like sheep without a shepherd.[37]
>
> Then he said to his disciples, "the harvest is plentiful, but the laborers are few;[38] pray therefore the Lord of the harvest to send out laborers into his harvest."
>
> 10:16, "Behold, I send you out as sheep in the midst of wolves; so be wise as serpents and innocent as doves."

The disciples of Christ have been clearly mandated to go in Christ's name, under Christ's authority, to carry out Christ's mission. They are to hold before people a vision of a world made new, a world fashioned after God's own heart; the Kingdom of God. The disciples were called to deal with the profound needs of human beings according to the foundation laid down by Jesus Christ in his life and ministry. Pastoral care, therefore, is an essential and core part of what we are about as the Church. Pastoral care assumes no superiority in the person of the pastoral caregiver in relation to the recipient. All persons stand in the same loving relationship to a loving God.

Reconciliation is foundational to pastoral care. We have been reconciled to God through Jesus Christ, therefore we all have this ministry of reconciliation. Our work is to help others become reconciled to God, with themselves, and in reference to their fellow human beings. St. Paul wrote in II Corinthians 5:17-20 (NRSV).

> "Therefore, if anyone is in Christ, they are a new creation; the old has passed away, behold the new has come.[18] All this is from God, who through Christ reconciled us to himself and gave us the ministry of reconciliation.[19] That is, in Christ God was reconciling the world to himself, not counting their trespasses against them, and intrusting to us the message of reconciliation.[20] so we are ambassadors of Christ, God is making his appeal through us. We beseech you on behalf of Christ, he reconciled to God."

There are different gifts of the Spirit dispersed among all the people of God. There are differing gifts that correspond to the different functions, which need to be fulfilled in the Church and world. All of these gifts in all of the people must be honoured. They derive from the one Spirit. There is, however, a higher and indispensable gift given to all God's people. That gift is the gift of love. Without this gift the ministry of Jesus Christ becomes a mechanical mockery. Paul writes in I Corinthians 13:1-3:

> "If I speak in the tongues of men and of angels, but have not love, I am a noisy gong or a clanging cymbal.[2] And if I have prophetic powers, and understand all mysteries and all knowledge, and if I have all faith, so as to remove mountains, but have not love, I am nothing.[3] If I give away all that I have, and if I deliver my body to be burned, but have not love, I gain nothing."

The life of a disciple of Christ must be grounded in a profound faith in God; and in a self-giving love toward all varieties of persons. Much pastoral care involves listening in understanding love. Jesus listened to many persons with understanding love. He reflected deeply upon what he heard. The parables he told are a testimony to his ability to understand human nature in a profound way; and to hold up a mirror before people so they might see themselves as God see them. Much of what Jesus said and did is, of course, not in the Gospel account. What we have is a condensation. There are situations that arise in pastoral care situations upon which the Gospels have nothing to say; i.e. high tech ethical decisions or blended families.

But in another way the Gospels give us a complete revelation of the meaning of pastoral care. They reveal quite clearly the spirit of Jesus in relation to persons and their needs. We see in Christ the manifestation of the Holy Spirit of God. Jesus was completely dedicated to showing forth the love of God in his love of people and the whole of creation. In John 20:21, we read:

> "As God has sent me, so I send you."

As the Disciples of Christ this is our mandate. The source of our love and caring is to be the love of God; as it was for Jesus. The direction of our pastoral ministry is clear. It is to be directed toward the needs of people. Our task is always forever to reveal, within the limits of our humanity, God's longing for our full, unencumbered flowering.

Pastoral care involves engaging in suffering love with another when there is the need. In suffering with people and for them in love they are helped to bear what they must bear and helped to find God's solution for their problems. We are called to deep empathy with others, feeling their pain, their anxiety, guilt, and emotional turmoil without violating their integrity; their selfhood. Jesus did not exploit or manipulate people in order to make them fit into some preconceived idea of who they were. He gave people the freedom to be, while at the same time living in such a transparent way that people could see what they might become.

We must always remember that the pastoral ministry is not our personal ministry. It is the ministry of Jesus Christ through the Holy Spirit at work through us; constant self-examination in the light of Christ's Spirit as revealed in the Gospels is of tantamount importance.

Personal prejudices, ego needs, or hostilities have no place in proper pastoral care. We must be always vigilant that we are not harming rather than healing. To meet another person in the name of Christ is a sacred trust. "Inasmuch as you have done it unto one of the least of these, you have done it unto me" Matt. 25:40 (NRSV).

This has profound spiritual implications of the pastoral ministry. The model for the Christian pastoral caregiver is the Spirit of Jesus Christ. It is this model rather than a strict adherence to the letter of the law that offers to all persons, regardless of any distinguishing feature whatsoever, profound honour and respect. All people have an undefiled and legitimate standing as a full, equal, and dearly beloved children of the living God. We have no mandate from Christ to rob anyone of this divine inheritance. As pastoral care workers it is part of our duty to see to it that no one in our care is diminished or desecrated for any reason whatsoever. We are to behave in a way that ferociously defends the inherent right of all persons to dignity, privacy, and self-determination in reference to God's will for their lives.

Pastoral care is always in response to God's love. We must know our proper role as instruments of this love. We are not God. God is God. So be it.

Freedom of Conscience

Anton T. Boisen has been identified as the father of clinical pastoral education. Many would say that he is the father of modern pastoral theology. He asserted that theological students should read "living human documents" in addition to the classical texts of theology. For Boisen, love of God and love of one's neighbour are foundational. The best way to approach the moral character of love in Boisen's thought is through his understanding of God's love as revealed through the crucifixion. He writes:

> That death upon the cross represents to me the love which is ready to give itself to the uttermost for the imperfect and the erring, a love that respects the integrity of each individual and refuses to coerce or to require obedience to the end that all may be bound together not through fear and through force but by the free response of love.[2]

Freedom of conscience has been a cornerstone of Protestant theology for centuries. It was one of the main issues of the Protestant Reformation. A human being's freedom to follow one's conscience has been seen as the source of their true dignity. Conscience is understood as the voice of God speaking to us immediately from within our own consciousness of ourselves. There is no need for any interference from any outside mediator in the form of a priest, a minister, or anyone else.

Ironically, centuries after the Reformation, the Catholic Church, when teaching on "freedom of conscience" stated in the councilor documents of Vatican II these words:

> Humans have in their hearts a law written by God. To obey it is the very dignity of the human; according to it we will be judged. Conscience is the most secret core and sanctuary of the human. There, we are alone with God, whose voice echoes in our depths. In a wonderful manner conscience reveals the law which is fulfilled by the love of God and your fellow humans. In fidelity to conscience Christians are joined to the rest of humanity in the search for truth, and for the genuine solution to the numerous problems that arise from the life of the individual and from social relationships.[3]

I am reminded of Paul's beautiful words found in 1 Corinthians 13:4-5,

> "Love is patient and kind; love is not jealous or boastful; it is not arrogant or rude. Love does not insist on its own way..."

When we in the Church are offering pastoral care in the name of Jesus Christ, we must have a profound respect for the other as a divine creation with a unique and precious eternal destiny. Our foundational posture should always be one of humility before the unknown, a lack of arrogance or rudeness, and a willingness to listen and, if necessary, learn. People long to speak their truth and to be truly heard.

People come to clergy for help and not for judgment, shaming, or rejection. An atmosphere of safety is paramount.

Traditionally, homosexuality was referred to in the Churches as "the sin that dare not speak its name". This silencing on the part of the Church has caused lesbian women to fear the Church and kept them from speaking their truth. Many lesbians 'live in the closet' and live out a 'masked self'. "Gay people who live in fear can so deny and repress their own thoughts and feelings until both wither up and they lose touch with their real identity."[4]

The Church has traditionally regarded itself as a defender of the Truth. It has been it's guardian and disseminator. This has been it's raison d'être. To tell the truth "gladly" has been the whole purpose of the Church. The very nature of Truth, however, is that it is not, at present, in its final form. There are always new discoveries, new realities to grapple with. Some of the truths we believed before have become "uncouth" with the passage of time, as persons speak of their experience of life, and scientists make new discoveries.

Thomas Gertler, S.J. writes:

> I have always experienced the Church as the place where more freedom, more openness and more preparedness for truth existed than in society at large. May it never come to pass that we lose this familiar Church, a Church in which we have such a foundational relationship of trust. May it never come to pass that there remain only isolated individuals in the Church with whom...I can speak my innermost truth and know that it will be received with love and reverence. May the Church itself as an institution in all humility always place itself at the disposal of truth, which is greater even than the Church itself.[5]

The central Christian teaching of freedom of conscience is based on Jesus' promise to his followers to send them the Holy Spirit who will live and dwell in their hearts. The Holy Spirit is democratic in nature. In the Acts of the Apostles on Pentecost Sunday, Peter recalls these words of the prophet Joel: "I shall pour out my spirit on all humanity. Your sons and your daughters shall prophesy, your young people shall see visions, your old people dream dreams. Even on the slaves, men and women, shall I pour out my Spirit." (Acts 2:17-18; Joel 3:1-2) In John 16:13 we read: "When the Spirit of truth comes he will lead you to the complete truth." Paul envisioned this Spirit as the author and source of the glorious freedom of the children of God. He writes in Galatians 5:1-2, "Christ has set us free, so that we should remain free. Stand firm, then, and do not let yourselves be fastened again to the yoke of slavery."

In Romans 8:14-17, Paul again writes: "All who are guided by the Spirit of God are sons and daughters of God; for what you have received was not the spirit of slavery to bring you back into fear; you received the Spirit of adoption, enabling us to cry out, 'Abba, Father!' The Spirit himself joins with our spirit to bear witness that we are the children of God. And if we are children, then we are heirs, heirs of God...."

Maurice Blondel gives philosophical expressions to this same theme of freedom to live one's truth when he says, "Our God dwells within us, and the only way to become one with our God is to become one with our authentic self."[6]

When Jesus left the disciples they were forced to mature into the fullness of their personhood; with the aid and guidance of the Holy Spirit. We too are called to that same journey of trust and faith and authenticity. We cannot always depend upon outside authorities, who themselves are part of fallible humanity, to tell us how we should conduct our lives. The question should always be: "As a dearly beloved child of God and heir with Christ how am I to conduct my unique and precious life?" Always grateful for the advice and insight of others, our lives are ours to live. Our sexuality is an integral part of our humanity and a gift from God. No person should have to experience this gift as a curse, when God has meant it as a blessing. No one has the right to cloak another in shame when that person is trying to respond to the truth of their innermost being. No one has the right to silence another and call it love in the name of Christ. And no one should live in fear because the Church finds their truth too disruptive of established norms.

Basic, healthy, faithful pastoral care, it would seem to me, consists of a willingness to allow God to be different from the way we had formerly thought. This is evidenced in the people who came for unconditional love and caring from the Church. Basic pastoral care for me requires an adventurous spirit; one that is not threatened by the new and untrodden paths. Basic pastoral care provides an atmosphere of safety whereby a person does not feel terror at the thought of detection if they do not think or act in ways that were previously accepted as norms.

Our God is a creative God. Everyday is a new creation. Every person is a new creation. If we impose upon persons paradigms from a previous understanding we destroy the creation in some way. God is not allowed to "do a new thing". Pastoral care is about setting a person free to be the person they were meant to be; free from the shackles and ignorance of the past. The image is one of sculpture emerging from a stone; gradually set free from all that does not belong to its truth.

In the name of Christ let us, as we offer pastoral care in the Church, be true liberators of our brothers and sisters and not their source of shame, degradation and slavery. The Church is not Big Brother.

CHAPTER TWO

A Brief History of the Gay Liberation Movement

Historically the "Gay Liberation" movement is very young. At the end of the last century and in the early 1900's Magnus Hirshfeld and the Institute of Sexual Sciences did much pioneering work in Germany, which resulted in homosexual flowering and liberation. However, the rise of Adolf Hitler brought all these advances to a sudden and violent halt. Hirshfeld was discredited, and the Institute and its library were destroyed. The homosexual persons in Germany were marked with a pink triangle, and it is believed that during this period in history about 250,000 homosexual persons were exterminated.[7]

Following World War II there began to emerge, in places like New York City, a climate of understanding and compassion for homosexual persons. Dr. Alfred A. Cross, along with others in New York City, chartered the George W. Henry Foundation in 1947. Its mandate was not to force homosexual persons to become heterosexual, but to offer them support and understanding. In the 50's most groups that formed in support of homosexual persons met secretly behind closed doors and drew the shades.[8]

The impetus for the Gay "Liberation Movement" as we know it today came as a result of what we now term, "The Stonewall Riot". This took place in Greenwich Village, New York City in June of 1969. A homosexual bar was being raided by the police. Previously, the clientele meekly subjected themselves to the bullying and degrading behaviour of the police, but on this particular occasion they had had enough and they fought back. The arresting police were forced to barricade themselves in the bar until they could be rescued. There was intense rioting for three days. Homosexual persons had decided it was time for a change. The tide turned in the hearts and minds of countless homosexual persons, and as a result the ramifications from that day reverberate to this day. Courage was born. Pride was born.[9] Refusal to be denied human rights was born. People in countless numbers refused to hide in closets of fear and shame anymore. The prisoners were set free. Refusal to be shackled by another's prejudice and ignorance is still evident today. Gay Pride marches happen in all the major cities every year in North America. Homosexual persons do not hesitate to go to court for their right to full and equal citizenship. The struggle is not over. There is a long, long way to go; but the exodus from the Egypt of terror and fear has begun.

CHAPTER THREE

Pastoral Care Issues for Lesbian Women

Grief and Loss

We are all on the journey of life. William Wordsworth has said all of us are "travelers between life and death." All of us must deal with loss and with grief at various points along this journey. The Church has traditionally helped, through its pastoral care, during those times in life when people are in the process of letting go; and when they are in distress and grief. Second Corinthians (1:3-4) describes this journey well: "Blessed be the God and Father of our Lord Jesus Christ, the Father of all mercies and the God of all consolation, who consoles us in our affliction with the consolation with which we ourselves are consoled by God." The bereaved person is consoled so they can turn again and console another. We are equipped as members of the Church to carry out a ministry of caring and consolation.[10]

Grief has many causes and many facets. There is grief at the loss of a spouse, a sibling, a parent, a home, an occupation, a friend, status, self-esteem, a child, health, a community, a sense of purpose, etc. This grief may take the form of anger, guilt, loneliness, humour, self-deceit, depression, acting-out, lethargy, and decline of health and withdrawal. Grief is a difficult thing to deal with and it is a very real part of our human journey. Most ministers deal with the grief of their parishioners on an ongoing basis, as does the caring Christian community. They are there to support and help the person through the crisis and to help them make the adjustment to normal functioning. For most people grief is episodic and transitory. Some people have longer recovery periods than others, but for the most part people are able to move on with their lives. All spiritual growth involves a mourning process. This process moves through the developmental stages of life and faces the inevitable losses of life, ie. parents. Religious faith is a tremendous bulwark against despair in the face of loss. It becomes essential to have some relationship with the Divine in life's moments of loss.

Unfortunately, for the lesbian person the Church, rather than being a source of comfort and strength, has instead become a place of condemnation too frequently. It uses, too often, scripture to condemn homosexuality and is a perpetrator of much of the grief and loss that the lesbian person must bear; over and above the expected losses of life. This grief and loss are not episodic and transitory; but rather chronic and part of the very fabric of the life of most lesbian persons.

John McNeill writes:

> In my twenty years as a pastoral counselor and psychotherapist to lesbians and gays, I have found that the chief threat to the psychological and spiritual health of most gay people, especially those coming from a strong Christian background, is guilt with its companions shame and low self-esteem, which can in turn develop into self-hate. The danger of destructive guilt and shame has always accompanied every step of gay and lesbian human development.... To live with an unconscious burden of guilt, shame, and self-hate is to live under continual stress....[T]his continual stress can take

years off one's life. Unrelieved emotional stress can produce high blood pressure, ulcers, strokes, heart attacks, colitis, asthma, allergic responses, and immune deficiency.[11]

A person who is not heterosexual in this culture and in this society bears an overwhelming burden of grief and loss. First, there is the realization that their life will be shrouded in shame no matter what their accomplishments, so there is a great loss of joy and celebration in the gift of life. There is a loss of a sense of belonging in the way heterosexuals belong.

John McNeill writes:

> "To let go of the myth of belonging in this world is in some ways to have already undergone the mourning process that most people undergo at death." The result of that process is a growing spiritual freedom to live authentically and fearlessly in this world."[12]

Upon the realization of otherness the lesbian person is catapulted into an inevitable mourning process. This mourning process too often involves the loss of friends, family, hopes, dreams, an envisioned future, a sense of aliveness, and a sense of safety. Life has taken a sudden turn. Shock is often its accompaniment.

> Coming out as a lesbian in our culture... means a loss of privilege and protection and to open oneself to internal terrors and social risks that literally can be deadly. Lesbians.... Are not simply fighting to understand and accept inner meaning in their lives; they are fighting against an external system of hatred of the care of their humanity and an internalized self-denigration.... To affirm one's homosexuality and to live openly and joyfully with it is to lose status and to launch into a perilous future. It is not possible to face these losses alone. In addition to enormous personal courage, considerable social support is required."[13]

This social support is rarely found in the Church where, if it is not actively promoting intolerance toward lesbians and gays, is rarely actively proactive in creating a safe and supportive environment. Most liberal Churches while purporting to accept lesbians rarely acquaint themselves with the grief and loss issues involved, and are happy to leave things at a tolerance level. Mere tolerance is an insult when vast inequities of privilege exist.

Pastoral care, if it is to be pastoral care by the clergy and the lay members of our congregations, must be cognizant of the burden of grief and shame most lesbians carry, and tailor their pastoral care appropriately. It is not enough to label them deviants and class them with all manner of the dregs of society and then blithely retort: "All people are welcome here; Jesus ministered to all kinds of sinners." Lesbian people have had their dignity and honour ripped from their very being through ignorance, and it is not enough to allow that situation of indignity and injustice to continue without active protest in the name of love. Whenever anyone in God's world has been shorn of their dignity because of their race, creed, colour, or sexual orientation it behooves the Church to remember that we are one in Christ.

Pastoral care is no lily-livered thing that pats the suffering person on the head and says, "there, there". It is instead a full-bodied force to be reckoned with. It confronts the powers that oppress and it sets the captive free. Relational justice demands that as Christians we go through the painful process of self-examination to see if we are harbouring any residual prejudice against any group of people. Have we been part of the forces of oppression? We must be willing to lend our strength to their battle for freedom and justice. The words of Martin Luther King, Jr. ring in our ears: "Free at Last! Free at Last! Thank God Almighty! Free at Last! Countless white people joined forces with the black people to secure their freedom and dignity because they felt it was their Christian duty to resist injustice. That was pastoral care. Pastoral care is an activity, a movement, a challenging of the status quo when necessary.

What gay people ultimately have to give up is attachment to rejection and the need for people to affirm their wholeness and loveableness. It works like this: if you can't get confirmation of your wholeness and your rightful place in the universe from people... you look beyond them. You have no choice but to go someplace more cosmic.

> If you give up denying, fighting, and wallowing in the oppression, you stop being stuck in the mud... You begin to understand what Jesus meant when he said, "Mine is not a kingdom of this world." (Jn.18:36)[14]

Many Churches assert that the primary purpose of human sexuality is procreation and thereby dismiss homosexuality as non-generative. But human lovemaking has many more functions, such as communion with another, soothing, restoration, belonging, security, joyful play and sharing to name but a few. Then there is the assertion that one sex is not complete without the other opposite sex. This argument implies that we are not unique persons in our own right with a unique divine destiny. This argument rests upon sex-role stereotyping, which is often a cultural construct having nothing to do with our inherent nature. Besides, science has told us for years that we are androgynous creatures who commune with one another out of our fullness of being not our lack thereof.

There is a position on homosexuality officially subscribed to by several Church bodies at the present time. It holds that while homosexuality as an orientation is contrary to God's created intention, the homosexual person ought not to be adversely judged or rejected by the Church....

While this is a more tolerant and compassionate view than outright condemnation, it places lesbians in two impossible binds. One is... the internal recognition that one's own sexual orientation is as natural and fundamental as skin colour. It is both naïve and cruel to tell a lesbian woman, "your sexual orientation is unnatural and a perversion, but this is no judgment upon you as a person." The individual knows otherwise.

The other kind concerns the Churchly pressure toward celibacy. When the Church presumes to be nonjudgmental toward homosexual orientation but then prohibits genital expression, it is difficult to understand how the sense of guilt, even in the celibate, will be significantly alleviated. In most lesbians and gay men it is likely and understandable that anger will increase, for they will see this as a Churchly hypocrisy.[15]

Anger

Pastoral care of lesbians will, of necessity, have to involve the healthy handling of anger. One of the greatest challenges facing a lesbian person is how to cope with the anger that results from frequent and ongoing marginalization in the family, the society, and the Church. The anger seeps and settles into all the nooks and crannies of their lives and can erupt in neurotic and self-destructive ways. Injustice and denial of legitimate rights and opportunities can foment anger. This anger often becomes toxic because there does not seem to be any appropriate outlet. The anger that is internalized often becomes depression. It also often becomes fury against God.

Traditionally, many Christians were brought up to believe that the expression of anger was not appropriate Christian behaviour. Good Christians never got angry, and never hated anyone. All angry feelings were to be repressed and denied. Of course, Jesus was angry the Temple; but that was a special case and that was Jesus. The message was: anger is a sin.

> "The primary mechanism of denial that most of us instinctively use, adults as well as children, is… the 'Keeping Mother Good Syndrome'." The child is absolutely dependent upon the goodness and love of the parenting figure. If the mother is not good and loving, then the infant experiences anger and frustration. However, the child becomes fearful that this anger will drive the mother away. For the child, to lose mother would be like losing life itself. Thus the child will strive instinctively to deny and suppress any feelings of anger. The best way children have of doing this is to lower their self-image and direct their anger toward themselves: "I must have

been very bad to make mother so angry at me." Once a child has learned this mechanism for dealing with anger, there is a tendency to handle anger in this way for the rest of his or her life. When in later life such a person is treated badly, he or she does not get angry at the mistreating person, but directs the anger inward toward him or herself."[16]

Countless lesbians were brought up in the bosom of Mother Church. They were baptized as babies and loved and nurtured by the extended family of the Church. What a shock to realize that the ritual of belonging and equality is not for you, because you are not heterosexual. What a shock to feel the repugnance and rejection of people whom you have known and loved all these countless Sundays when the love of God in Jesus Christ was taught and lived in so many ways. What a heartache to find yourself shut out, the door closed until you twist your nature to suit theirs. First there is the shock, the heartache and despair, and then the anger and fury welling up from within. What to do with this anger, this grief, the powerlessness becomes the question.

St. Paul wrote, "Even if you are angry, you must not sin: never let the sun set on your anger or else you will give the devil a foothold." (Ephesians 4:26-27). By this we can understand, firstly, that anger is not sin but if it is not released it can lead to sinful behaviour and hostility. "Herein lies one of the great secrets of anger: anger that is experienced as powerful is easily dealt with, but anger that is experienced as powerless can easily turn into real hatred."[17]

In other words, it is very important for a person to give themselves permission to feel all their feelings whether they are positive or negative rather than "stuffing" them. Anger needs to be expressed. Unexpressed anger increases stress and can lead to all manner of stress-related diseases, eg. heart attacks. [Anger] is a natural, inevitable response to frustration or deprivation. Just as pain follows a physical wound, anger occurs when we feel we are being dealt with unjustly. Anger can be defined as psychic pain.[18] Lesbian people carry a great deal of it due to the societal context of their lives and the lack of conscious awareness by others who operate from a position of heterosexual privilege. Pastoral care involves helping the lesbian person cope with the inevitable anger through appropriate means of expression. A listening ministry is especially healing in this instance as the lesbian person feels silenced so frequently; often for self-protection.

Repressed or unexpressed anger builds walls between people. It kills and destroys intimacy and can lead to such behaviours as verbal abuse and withholding of positive regard and affection. Lesbian intimacy is very much affected by repressed anger and often spills over into unhealthy and distant patterns of relating. The very partner a person needs and desires is kept from offering the love and support they would normally give had the partner been more receptive. This dynamic places a severe strain on lesbian intimate relationships and fuels further anger and despair when there is a break up or an estrangement. There is also tremendous strain and angst on the part of both intimate partners when they must watch their partner, whom they love and cherish, deal with the prejudice and disqualifying behaviour of others. It not only provokes anguish to watch one's intimate other suffer, it provokes anger; anger that must not be allowed to turn to hatred or to be repressed and internalized.

Just as traditionally people have been taught that anger is bad or wrong when directed at other people, so many have been taught that it is wrong to be angry with or express anger to God. Our spiritual life is an effort to develop an intimacy with God. Anger is part of that intimacy as it is part of our intimacy with our fellow human beings. If, however, we do not feel the freedom and right to be angry with God then there is a wall between us and the intimacy dies.[19]

Pastoral care in this instance would involve helping the person to understand that they have every right to express their anger towards God who loves them unconditionally and longs to commune with, and help them. If this does not happen a person's spiritual life will become a wasteland, and much-needed strength and support will not be accessible. Many, many lesbians believe that God hates them and wants nothing to do with them. The fact that a representative of the Christian community would spend time with them and hold them in positive regard is in itself a balm to wounds too deep and painful to even speak of. The ministry of presence is of tantamount importance when extending pastoral care to this sector of the population.

> "For many gay people, dealing with the Church is like dealing with parents. Even if we seriously disagree with them and see what they have done to us as truly destructive, we still love them and are grateful for what they have done for us and given us. But that love does not negate the fact that we have been wounded by them, and as long as we remain wounded, there is unavoidable anger. The only healthy way to let go of that anger is to heal the wounds of self-hatred and self-rejection and strive to achieve an attitude of positive self-acceptance."[20]

Since lesbian people experience their orientation as a given and not as a willful choice in rebellion against God they experience perplexity and anger at a God who created them in the first place and then, through the Church, rejects and often despises them. Many people do not distinguish between God and the Church, the humanly fallible institution. Because of this they are unable to enjoy a spiritual life. The relationship with God is toxic and aborted and fuels tremendous anger in the person. Proper pastoral care must address this issue.[21]

The Families-of-Origin of Lesbian Women

Many parents, in fact, most parents, do not know how to handle the situation when their daughter reveals to them that they are not heterosexual, but prefer a same-sex partner. In their book, "Parents of the Homosexual", David Switzer and Shirley Switzer write that for most parents this revelation fills them with intense feelings of shame and guilt. They don't want anyone to find out and they keep wondering if it was caused by something they did wrong. Most parents and family members share the expectation of the rest of the society that children will grow up heterosexual, probably marry, and probably have children. This is a social ideal deeply embedded in all of the institutions of our society.[22]

> "....Failure to be this ideal is a part of the homosexual person's own grappling with identity and feelings of shame, feeling bad about one's self, having the very low self-esteem that is such a characteristic part of the reactions of these persons to the growing awareness of their sexual orientation, at least during the early stages and for some for a much longer period of time. Being linked together as we are in families, and often enough tending to look at families as a single entity within which differences are not expected, other persons feel shame also. Therefore, homosexuality, like a variety of other "family failures" (alcoholism and metal illness, for example), is to be kept a secret. Other people must never know, or we will all be social outcasts."[23]

Because of the intensity of the impact on the family of a homosexual family member an organization was formed to help and support these families. It is known as P-Flag or Parents and Friends of Lesbians and Gays. Most of the groups are in major cities are not available to people in smaller centers. The groups are listed in the telephone book. Gracious ministry needs to be offered to all family members by the clergy as representatives of a loving creative God.

Every family is different. Every family handles problems and stressful situations differently, but regardless of their differences most families move through a series of responses that are chronological. These responses are the stages of grief.[24]

The first stage is shock and denial. "The radical change in [the lives of the parents], the disruption of their dreams, and for most, the terrible pain of it usually produce a reaction of shock, a sense of unreality, or no feeling. Occasionally there may be intense anger, which can be a way of denying the other feelings the parent may be experiencing."[25]

The next stage is yearning. This period can last for a few weeks or months. The shock wears off, the reality cannot be denied, and the anger diminishes. The parents grieve in ways that resemble grief in the face of death. The person is still alive, however, and yet not the person they thought they were. The parents' dreams and expectations, both conscious and unconscious have been destroyed. In the minds of all of us, the dreams and expectations of a loved one, the one whom we would like for the person to be and thus believe the person to be, become merged with who that person really is. So with the loss of many of not most of those dreams and illusions, it feels as if the person they knew was dead. The parents are grieving in ways similar to grief in a loss by death. The difference is that the person is still alive and we have to do something with them.[26]

There is a yearning or an aching for what was. In their minds they go over and over the various stages in the development of their child.[27] Memories of childhood and adolescence flash on the screen of their minds. Dreams and images of a future now lost are grieved and worry about the life of inevitable suffering and heartache their child will have to face in a hostile and punitive society. They grieve for what lies ahead, powerless to stop the future they know will be far different from the one they envisioned.

Blaming often emerges at this stage. Blaming their child for "doing this to them", blaming influential adults in the child's life, blaming society, and blaming themselves. There is often a futile search for the things they did wrong, eg. "If only I had been home more". This process has no end and is ultimately totally unhealthy and non-productive.[28]

The parents at this stage resemble a person who is drowning, who is reaching for anything to save his/her life. Anything to return to the normal state-of-affairs.

The fourth stage is the transitional stage. "This stages is characterized by a diminishing of the intensity of most or all the feelings that parents have experienced; letting go of their dreams; attempting to see their son or daughter realistically; trying to learn more about homosexuality and what they are experiencing; perhaps seeing a minister or another counselor if they have not done so; beginning to give up trying to change their child's sexual orientation."[29]

There is not so much distress at this stage and the parents are able to focus on other things. There is still sadness and longing for what "could've been", but it is less consuming. Some parents may never move beyond this stage. There is an uneasy truce reached in some instances. In others, the parents completely separate from their child.[30]

The final stage, if it is achieved, is that of resolution – reconciliation....

"Many parents do come to an acceptance of the reality of their child's sexual orientation. They may feel entirely all right about it, or they may feel some longing and sorrow at times. But they have passed beyond anger, blaming themselves and others, no longer feeling guilty, no longer accusing their daughter or son."[31]

The ultimate goal, of course, is a relationship where all participants love and accept one another just as they are. These relationships should be characterized by complete honesty, joy in one another's unique being, and forgiveness. This of course, includes the siblings in any family grouping.[32]

Reaction: Lack of Hospitality

"He came to Nazareth, where he had been brought up, and went into the synagogue on the Sabbath day as he usually did. He stood up to read and they handed him the scroll of the prophet Isaiah. Unrolling the scroll he found the place where it is written: "The spirit of the Lord has been given to me, for he has anointed me. He has sent me to bring good news to the poor, to proclaim liberty to the captives and to the blind new sight, to set the downtrodden free, to proclaim the Lord's year of favor." He then rolled up the scroll, gave it back to the assistant and sat down. And all eyes in the synagogue were fixed on him. Then he began to speak to them, "This text is being fulfilled today even as you listen." Luke 4:16-21

Hospitality is a central virtue in both the Old and the New Testaments. A central commandment to Moses on Mt. Sinai was: "You must not molest the stranger or oppress him, for you lived as strangers in the land of Egypt (Ex. 22:20-21). In Genesis 18, Abraham is considered good and holy because of his hospitality to strangers. He is sitting in front of his tent one day and sees strangers passing by in the desert; he rushes out to implore them to accept his hospitality. He gives them water, washes their feet and provides them with a meal. In the harshness and inhospitality of the desert environment the caring of another could mean life or death. It turns out that Abraham is entertaining angels and he did not know it.[33]

When these angelic strangers pass on to Sodom, Lot's approval by God rests upon his hospitality to these men, in sharp contrast with his neighbours. He invites them to his home and provides them with food and lodging. "The primary message of the story of Sodom is that God will bless those who are kind and hospitable to strangers – not that homosexual acts are sinful. The prophet Ezekiel makes clear what the true sin of Sodom was: "The crime of your sister Sodom was pride, gluttony, arrogance, complacency; such were the sins of Sodom and her daughters. They never helped the poor and the needy...."[34]

Hospitality is also a central theme of the New Testament when we examine such passages as Matthew 10:14-15: Jesus is instructing the disciples in ministry and says, "If anyone does not welcome you or listen to what you have to say, as you walk out of the house shake the dust from your feet. I tell you solemnly, on the day of judgment it will not go as hard with the land of Sodom and Gomorrah as with that town." This text makes it clear that Jesus understood the paramount crime of Sodom was to be inhospitable to strangers. In response to the questions, "who is my neighbour?", Jesus responds with the story of the Good Samaritan, a person definitely on the margins of respectable Jewish society. He is teaching that the ministry of caring knows no limits or boundaries.

Luke 24: 13-35 tells the story of the disciples, after the horror of the crucifixion, walking along the road to Emmaus, emotionally drained and trying to find some meaning in the whole experience. Their spirits are lifted by a stranger who draws along beside them and elucidates the scriptures in such a way that their sense of meaninglessness and despair evaporate like the dew. When they reach the end of their journey this stranger is more than prepared to move along and not prevail upon them in any way. The disciples, who could easily have let the stranger go on due to their own deep need for rest, instead strongly urge this stranger to share their hospitality. "When they break bread at table they recognize the risen Jesus.... The message here is that we encounter the divine by reaching out to our neighbour."[35]

The words of Christ in Matthew 25:40 "in so far as you did it to one of the least of these brothers [and sisters] of mine, you did it to me" form a foundational value system for all Christians. Hospitality to "the other" is an important practice in various Christian-based cultures. "In ancient Ireland every cottage would leave its door open and place food and drink by the fireplace and a candle in the window in case a stranger should pass by and need hospitality."[36]

We traditionally think of hospitality in terms of giving a good party but John McNeill states that hospitality is a state of mind and soul.

Henri Nouwen defines hospitality as "that virtue which allows us to break through the narrowness of our fears and open our home to the stranger with the understanding that salvation comes to us in the form of a tired traveler."[37]

Nouwen notes that in order to truly be hospitable a person must be totally at home in their own home and that a primary condition for true hospitality is that the host be totally present and not distracted by needs, worries, or anxieties. The "wholly other" deserves our full unselfish attention.[38] Countless lesbians down through the centuries have offered others the hospitality of their full personhood through various ministries and professions and continue to do so today in the face of societal shaming. John McNeill writes: "Positive gay pride is pride in our sense of hospitality and compassion."[39]

In his book, "The Church and the Homosexual", John McNeill traces the historical process by which a biblical condemnation of inhospitality was transformed into a condemnation of homosexuality. He writes:

> "Here is one of the supreme ironies of history: for thousands of years in the Christian West, homosexuals have been victims of, to say the least, inhospitable treatment – the true sin of Sodom – in the name of a mistaken understanding of Sodom's crime. That misunderstanding has traditionally focused on a sub-theme of the Sodom story, namely the practice in ancient Near Eastern religious of depersonalized sex to ensure fertility of the soil and secure the God's blessing. This aspect of the Sodom story was confused with the episode's central, positive theme: that God blesses those who are hospitable to strangers."[40]

CHAPTER FOUR

Finding A Place of Belonging in The Church

"And when Jesus had been baptized he at once came up from the water, and suddenly the heavens opened and he saw the Spirit of God descending like a dove and coming down on him. And suddenly there was a voice from heaven, 'This is my Son, the Beloved: my favour rests on him'." (Matthew 3:16-17)

These words of God are spoken to each and every one of us. Love has willed us into being. "We must remember that God does not create as a human artist creates. God does not will us into being and then forget us. If God were to forget us, we would cease to be. At every moment, the Spirit of God is birthing us out of love."[41]

The same voice that called out in love at the baptism of Jesus cries out to us as well. "You are my beloved, in whom I am well-pleased." How dare the Church allow our lesbian sisters to be called despicable and names too hurtful to repeat? Countless women have internalized these names and have retreated into the darkness and despair of self-rejection and shame. Guilt and low self-esteem become their constant companions. Darkness covers their lives with their families, friends, and fellow congregants to whom they are afraid to reveal themselves.

> "The Church has not been a healthy place for lesbians. But many lesbians have been raised by the Church, and while many have left the religion of their childhood and youth, it is hard to leave religion completely behind. This is especially true since biblical standards permeate Western society and Jewish and Christian belief systems undergird much of our cultural symbols, rituals, and mindset. Most lesbians who have stayed in the congregation have remained in the closet."[42]

> "For where two or three meet in my name, I shall be there with them." (Matthew. 18:20)

It is in this passage that Jesus emphasizes the importance of community in our lives. It was his intention that the Church would be a community of love and caring; where all people would be celebrated and all people cared for. St. Paul writes: "My brothers and sisters, you were called as you know to liberty; but be careful, or this liberty will provide an opening for self-indulgence. Serve one another, rather, in works of love, since the whole law is summarized in a single commandment: Love your neighbour as yourself. If you go snapping at each other and tearing each other to pieces, you had better watch or you will destroy the whole community." (Galatians 5:13-15).

It would seem to me that a person living in community has a right to be their natural self without fear of reprisal or marginalization. I do not believe Jesus would support communities where some people are allowed to be themselves and to fully flourish while others must cower and be content with third-class status and worse.

Gail Lynn Unterberger states that:

> "There can be no doubt that religious institutions have played a powerful role in the oppression of lesbians to a greater or lesser extent in history...

Religion has given theological, biblical, and doctrinal arguments to undergird homosexuals' status as social pariahs, sexual deviants, loathsome, and the worst of all sinners in the eyes of God. And religion has depicted lesbians as more degraded, depraved, promiscuous, and damnable than heterosexual women."[43]

Many scholars from the various disciplines of sociology, anthropology, biology, psychology, psychiatry, ethics are in the process of a major overhaul of their understandings of human sexuality. This is challenging traditional Church stances. Several mainline Churches are currently in the process of re-evaluating their official statements. This is good news for countless lesbians and people of various gender orientations who have too long suffered in silence, shame, and isolation.

In a relationship when one person has to de-self themselves in order to stay in that relationship both people lose the richness and growth potential of that relationship. When a lesbian person must hide their true identity, concerns, and struggles in order to be a dignified member of a congregation, then both parties are the losers. The lesbian person lives in terror of discovery and its consequences, and is thereby operating out of a false-self. Lesbians learn very early on how to pretend to be heterosexual. They learn to "pass". They may refer to boyfriends past or present. They may even marry seeking to conform to societal expectations, and/or as a way to put heterosexuals "off the scent". Many remain celibate and alone often serving in the capacity of beloved aunts and/or community workers in one form or another, eg. teachers, doctors, ministers, artists, therapists, secretaries, etc. Lesbians have been fitting into their various communities without detection for centuries. They have made a terrific contribution to families, schools, hospitals, the theatre, and all the arts. They deserve commendation rather than denigration. They deserve better than lives lived in secret shame. How dare the Church, which has benefited from the gifts of lesbian women in marvelous and wonderful ways, allow the lies and the unspeakable suffering to continue? It is not the lesbian persons who should bear the cloak of shame; it is the Church.

> "There are few well-known healthy role models for lesbians. Lesbians portrayed by the dominant literature, media, culture, and narratives are usually not sympathetic personalities, but are stereotypically depicted as unattractive, butch, bull-dykes, man-haters, 'witches', and more."[44]

We live in a world where people are becoming more and more isolated from one another. We are living a "fractured reality" and for many people for various reasons the Church is just not a place where they are finding loving community. For lesbian people who are not willing to live a life of deception this is most definitely true. The old heterosexist paradigms of family and Church are no longer working for them. They are tired of the exclusivness.

> "In most ecclesiastical and theological communities, it is ostensibly no longer tolerable to express racist views. It is also increasingly less fashionable to exhibit sexist beliefs and behaviours... Yet homophobia and heterosexism are rarely discussed, confronted, or confessed in the pulpit or Sunday School. The liberal Churches have failed utterly to take heterosexism seriously, and therefore have failed to do justice to women's lives "whether heterosexual, bisexual, genitally active, genitally inactive, or celibate."[45]

There is an ancient Hasidic story that emphasizes the value of a loving, authentic, healthy community. A good rabbi asked God to show him heaven and hell before he died. So God brought him into a room in the afterworld. In that room, a group of emaciated and unhappy people sat around a pot of food hanging over the fire. They were trying to feed themselves, but their efforts were in vain because their spoons were too long for them to place the food in their mouths. The rabbi was informed that this is hell. Then he was taken to an identical room with a similar group of people sitting around another pot of food with the same long spoons, but there was happiness and joy. The only difference was that they fed one another. The difference made this place heaven.[46] The difference in our Church communities when all people can feed one another from the bread of their authentic selves will be "marvelous in our eyes".

If the Church continues to deny lesbians an honoured place at the table of our Christian communities then the Church not only will be responsible for the rendering asunder of God's fabric of love, it will also lose the right and privilege of pastoring lesbian people. The Church is not God. There are countless lesbians who believe that God hates them because the Church hates them, or at least considers them second-class Christians. Their relationship with God has become extremely distorted and, in many cases, destroyed because of the moral pronouncements by the Church. People have a right to live free from the Church's condemnation. Many parts of the Church have taught that lesbians will not enter the kingdom of heaven and that they will burn in hell. John has written: "Love will come to its perfection in us when we can face the Day of Judgment without fear; because even in this world we have become as he is. In love there can be no fear, but fear is driven out by perfect love; because to fear is to expect punishment, and anyone who is afraid is still imperfect in love." (John 4:17-19).

We are very concerned in the Church with all forms of abuse all the way from child abuse, spousal abuse, to elder abuse. We are calling people to account and naming the abuse. Spiritual abuse is one we do not identify too often; but it is my contention that lesbian women have been subjected to spiritual abuse by the Church through the distorted use of scripture and the assumption that everyone's experience is heterosexuality. There has been a resounding lack of support in the Churches, regardless of where they fall on the theological spectrum, for anything but heterosexual relationships. The furor on all sides over the same-sex marriage issue bears testimony to this fact. Just as a therapist who is at all ethical should declare their homophobia before entering into the sacred soul of another; perhaps the Church should do the same. Too many lesbians thought they were in a safe space and found out quite differently, to their horror and heartache, that they were definitely not. A pastor who is convinced that homosexuality is disordered should respect the choice of the people involved. It is not their place to approve or disapprove; only to offer loving pastoral care.

The Book of Wisdom, Chapter 11:24-12:1 says: "Yes, you love all that exists, you hold nothing of what you have made in abhorrence, for had you hated anything, you would not have formed it. And how, had you not willed it, could a thing persist, how be conserved if not called forth by you? You spare all things because all things are yours, Lord, lover of life, you whose imperishable spirit is in all."

Some Christian Churches claim to love lesbian persons, but label them sinners and insist that they remain celibate. The rallying cry is, "hate the sin, love the sinner". The problem with this is a lack of understanding that a person's sexuality is not some sort of "add-on" that they can put on or take off at will. Sexuality is imbedded in our very being, so when a lesbian person is called a sinner because they are not heterosexual and told not to express their sexuality because it is abhorrent, then a severe contortion in the person's very being takes place. It is like saying to a person who has brown skin that until they become white they are a sinner and have no right to exist. This approach is highly destructive of the human psyche of the lesbian person. The tragedy is that well-meaning, highly committed Christians are taking this approach; believing with all their hearts that they are living out the Christian mandate to love their neighbour. They just cannot imagine that God's creation would include homosexual love as part of the diversity of creation.

All of us struggle with various issues at various stages and junctures in our lives…

> "It is crucial to note that in a hostile and predominately heterosexual world, lesbians' feeling of anger, rejection, and hurt can exacerbate whatever situational, emotional, or developmental crisis arises during the life cycle."[47]

Some are driven to suicide. All suffer unjustly. Many turn to alcohol and drugs to cope with the emotional pain and the lack of security in their lives. This draws further disdain from many in the Church who have no concept of what the lesbian woman is dealing with on a daily basis.

Many lesbian women have been driven from the Church and have fallen by the wayside. The words from the prophet Ezekiel have a message for the Church:

> "The word of the Lord came to me: "Son of man, prophesy against the shepherds of Israel; prophesy and say to them: "This is what the Sovereign Lord says: Woe to the shepherds of Israel who only take care of themselves! Should not shepherds take care of the flock? You eat the curds, clothe yourselves with the wool and slaughter the choice animals, but you do not take care of the flock. You have not strengthened the weak or healed the sick or bound up the injured. You have not brought back the strays or searched for the lost. You have ruled them harshly and brutally. So they were scattered because there was no shepherd, and when they were scattered over the whole earth, and no one searched or looked for them. Therefore, you shepherds, hear the word of the Lord: As surely as I live, declares the Sovereign Lord, because my flock lacks a shepherd and so has been plundered and has become food for all the wild animals, and because my shepherds did not search for my flock but cared for themselves rather than for my flock, therefore, O shepherds, hear the word of the Lord: This is what the Sovereign Lord says: I am against the shepherds and will hold them accountable for my flock. I will remove them from tending the flock so that the shepherds can no longer feed themselves. I will rescue my flock from their mouths, and it will no longer be food for them. For this is what the Sovereign Lord says: I myself will search for my sheep and look after them. As a shepherd looks after his scattered flock when he is with them, so will I look after my sheep. I will rescue them from all the places where they were scattered on a day of clouds and darkness." (Ezekiel 34:1-12)

CHAPTER FIVE

Research: The Stories

Betty's Tape

What is your connection with the Church?

Well my connection with the Church was that I was bought up Catholic and I was a good Catholic until I was thirteen. Then I slowly left the Church until I left home. Then after that I didn't go to Church anymore. So that is my connection with the Christian Church.

Why did you leave when you were around thirteen?

Because I didn't believe in what the Church was telling me. It wasn't a place that I cared to go. I just didn't believe in what they were trying to tell me. It was like I was questioning what they were trying to, in some ways forcing me, to believe. So, I think intellectually, it wasn't making any sense for me. It was, you know, just a matter of my questioning and not believing; but being in a household with a strong Catholic back ground, I had to comply with to the house rules. So I kept going to Church until I figured out how not to go to Church.

How would you describe your awakening to your lesbian identity?

Well the awakening was... it took... I didn't actually self identify as a lesbian, like Lesbian Pride until I was thirty. However, in hindsight I was probably identified as a lesbian when I was about fifteen. All my dreams, fantasies were all around women. It was good. Reflection is a basic. (Ha, ha, ha). So it was... but to actually feel comfortable and say that I was a lesbian it was seventeen years later. In looking back, I was a lesbian. I was a Jock. I hung out with girls and I really didn't care to hang out with guys. In hindsight, I was a lesbian a long, long time before I suffered anything. Yeah.

Were you able to share this identity with the people closest to you?

No. No, not at all! No, you mean just on the... I was... Well, when I was truly identified the people who were closest to me, at that point of time in my life when I was thirty, were friends as opposed to family and I was certainly able to share that with friends and very safely because they were mostly queer folk as well. So that worked out but it was never within my family but they weren't the closest to me then. So....

Did you suffer any losses or were you celebrated because of your Lesbian Identity?

Suffered any losses? I don't think I suffered losses because I don't disclose it to my family. So, I didn't suffer those losses because by not disclosing that it was just a guessing game on their part or they were just in denial. I know other lesbian women who just put themselves forward to their family and they were just cut off from the family. They were a threat to the family and so. I didn't do that. So I didn't have a tremendous loss. The celebration came within the community of friends. It was certainly a celebration because you start to identify with a community of gay and lesbian people and that was always a celebration, an openness. Certainly a celebration of the friends' side of my life. It wasn't until I was a lesbian, or self-identified as a lesbian, for about eight to nine years that my family started to use the word lesbian and became comfortable with the woman that I was with. So the family side sort of celebrated my homosexuality. Certainly it started when I was thirty-five and "othered". I wouldn't say celebrated as much as recognized it, as celebration is a bit of a stretch for my family. They certainly recognized it and I always felt welcomed as they welcomed the women in my life into my family. I never felt my siblings as being homophobic and my father and mother have always been welcoming for whoever I bring into the house. However, I have never stood in front of them and said, "I am a dyke. I am a lesbian and I want you to accept who I am." I never put them through that challenge. But they know.

So they don't really celebrate it, but they don't interfere?

Right, precisely, and that's a nice way to put it.

How has the Church offered you pastoral care as you came to recognize your Lesbian Identity?

Well, certainly the Church was never helpful. So it's always hindsight some of this stuff. So as I was getting out, leaving the Church at fifteen, you only can think and say, that well, if only they had celebrated the thought about homosexuality as being something as ok then I could really be in touch with my true feelings when I was just starting to be sort of showing signs of being a sexual being. It could have been a different thing. Maybe the Church could have spoken to who I was. Maybe they could have helped me to come out. Instead I stayed in the closet until I was thirty and not only the social closet; but also my own closet. So I would say the Church could have been extremely helpful and it was definitely a hindrance. There were no positive messages and everything was always – messages were always negative, were always just words that were disparaging remarks about homosexuality. So there was no encouragement to reflect on this in a positive way.

So that was a hindrance and very unsupportive and not an environment at all.

So it wasn't any help as you developed your lesbian relationships?

Well, it was not really a factor because I was not a Christian. So it's not like I was looking for any sort of support within a Christian or religious community. So it was never really a factor. The women I've been with were never that religious, that they were that connected to a Church, that I had to be involved with their religion. So that's what it was about.

How has the Church offered you pastoral care in painful times during your relationships – say during times of death or illness, break up, loss of a job?

Again the Church was never a factor. The Church has never been a factor in my life. So… but when I had to go to Church for like a wedding…the only time I will go to Church is when something's been asked of me. So I go to a wedding and the words within that wedding were very heterosexual. It's all about procreation and those kinds of attitudes. Not only is it a heterosexual wedding, but the messages were all around heterosexual messages like this coming in from the pulpit. So this like really frustrated me and just made me angry. So not only am I trying to be there, be supportive of a sibling or somebody getting married… you try not to get angry but you can't help but get angry and kind of perturbed at the messages around marriages, around procreation and heterosexuality. It's just frustrating and gives me all the more reason to just stay away.

What has been your experience of the Church's teachings in reference to human sexuality?

Well it seems that the teachings are… people seem to want to interpret them the way they wish to interpret them. So someone can take a teaching or a passage and interpret it as very homophobic and someone else can take it and interpret it as being very open and accepting. So I always found it as so broad and the human beings, wherever they should be coming from, in their own heads or in their own socialization. That they could use the Bible either as an incredible source of opposition by using the Bible and using it as their ally or people who would take the Bible and interpret it as a way of supporting a different type of sexuality; so that homosexuality was a hit. But mostly it seems the Bible is used by the homophobes and the fanatics to keep homosexuality out of society.

Was that your experience growing up? Did you hear that?

Well I certainly heard it in the younger years. Not because it wasn't such a social issue back when I was ten, twelve, thirteen. It was more like Communism was a social issue and they certainly used the Church to talk about the evils of Communism; and so it wasn't such a social problem back then. Quote "a social problem" is seen to begin the more the Queer Community wanted to be more "out" and be identified more as a family and that's when we became such a huge social problem which would be probably the 1970's and 1980's.

So would you say kind of an inherent teaching was that the family had to be heterosexual?

Oh, absolutely. Good heavens, there was absolutely no commission to use that word in any other way. Oh absolutely, yeah. It took a lot of work to broaden that word and so people can self-identify the family in a pretty broad sense. Oh yeah. There is a lot of ownership to that word. A lot of the heterosexual world has had ownership on a lot of language and a lot of social mores. They very much dictated and used the Bible to support it.

Have you felt free to take your partner to Church or do you feel you must hide your relationship?

No. Not now. Not in the last fifteen years. I don't hide anything. No, it's no longer an issue for me. I wish we could get this attitude for the world to accept me for who I am and what I am or don't accept me and I am going to be o.k. with it too. But I think it's more because of… oh… a few reasons: 1) because of age and 2) as a society we've moved tremendous leaps and bounds on the issue. So we have not only allies amongst the homosexual community that has came out; but all the siblings and all the parents and all the other people who are associated with those lesbian and gay people that also don't tolerate it. So this is obviously support in numbers and numbers are the issue in terms of saying we're living in a different time. You don't need to be afraid or concerned about who you are. You know it's like o.k. because we live in different times. So you're not the odd person out. It's the person that comes across as a homophobe that's the odd person now.

How do you experience your relationship with the Church at the present time?

I don't have a relationship with the Church. No relationship.

Is there anything you would like to say to the Church in reference to your Lesbian Identity?

Is it just to the Anglican Church, or to any Church?

Anything you would like to say to any Church?

Yes, certainly that the Churches need to use the teachings of people who have been the philosophers and leaders, whether they be Gods or Goddesses. We as humans should take those philosophical teachings and stories and apply them to human life. When we are applying them it's not about whom you're deciding is going to be your partner or family. It's not about them at all. It's just about the human condition of being on earth as opposed to anything else. It's not about your sexuality. It shouldn't be an issue. It's nothing to do with it, nothing at all. It's a red herring. It shouldn't even be bought up. For someone to bring it up it's absolutely silly. It's about being on earth and living here without or with harmony. Living with harmony and peace and not harming others. It has nothing to do with sexuality. As long as you're not hurting others.

Is there anything else you want to say?

Well, I guess it's one thing to say that sexuality is not an issue; but you have to get there first by talking about it. Just put it out there so it's not an issue. So I guess that's where we are right now, and unfortunately we have to talk about it. We have to get over it and we want to. We are not going to get over it until we have processed it and sorted it out in our minds as the human species that this is who we are. So, I think, we are sort of on that path of letting it go; but we are definitely still on the path. It's a process and processes are always long and you can't rush it. Yeah, so you just have to accept and be patient but not too patient. We don't have forever here, you know. There has to be a reasonable time line to deal with this in a manner that's expedient. When it gets to a place where it is resolved and then it's not an issue. We can look back at this and say, "Back in the year 2000 they were still dealing with human sexuality in this way." It will be barbaric. They will look back in a hundred years and think it was absolutely barbaric. It won't look good.

So o.k. and is that you final word?

Yes.

Yes, o.k. and thank you.

Pam's Tape

What has been your connection with the Church?

My only connection with the Church was basically when I was a kid and if I wanted to go to any Church, then I could go to any Church. Sometimes I got dragged to the Gospel Hall with my Grandfather. Sometimes I went to the United Church with friends. I've been to the Catholic, the Pentecostal, the Nazarene, and the Catholic Church. I've been in an awful lot of them, but joined nothing. I had gone up to the point when I was in C.G.I.T. and the question came down to if you were going to be a part of the Church then you had to be Baptized, and I wasn't Baptized. So I never went beyond that. That was the end.

How would you describe your awakening to your Lesbian Identity?

That's good – my awakening to my identity. I don't know if it was an awakening. Other than I just knew there was something there that I had to find out about really. I know I certainly got crushes on females and I'm talking, oh I guess, about ten, eleven. During around then.

Starting around ten or eleven you started having crushes on females?

Yes, but yet not really knowing what was going on. Not being too wise to the world at ten and eleven years of age, it probably... it wasn't until I read a novel and I don't remember what the novel was. So I probably would have been maybe twelve or thirteen... maybe even...no, maybe about twelve, thirteen. There was a lesbian scene in it and it really, really turned my crank. At that point I said, "Wow, this is something that I got to check out." That was probably the light really going on. However, being a small town, other than necking with your friends when you got into the 'hooch', when you weren't supposed to. When I left here I had full intentions and knew I would find out very soon, once I hit the big city, where things lurk.

So when you hit the 'big city', you?

Well because I was a member, I went into Psychiatric Nursing. So I was in residence. I was a nursing resident.

You went into Psychiatric Nursing and you were in Nurses' Residence?

I was in Nurses' Residence and it didn't take very long to find the right crowd… (ha, ha, ha). Within a matter of probably weeks, not much more, somebody said, "Well, let's party this weekend and do you want to come? I have to tell you it's a little different!" I said, 'Yeah, I'll be there." That was it then the beginning of it. I went and never looked back.

So your awakening really happened in Residence – Nurses' Residence? I mean, you know, full blown?

Well would I call it full blown? Well… yeah probably… certainly it was out of that my first sexual experience with a female… I mean other than the necking sessions…So yeah, yeah.

Were you able to share this identity, your lesbian identity, with those closest to you? Your family?

No. No, because this was back in the 1960s'. All I ever heard said in my house, and it was usually a reference when something had been in the news or in the newspaper about something a pedophile had done. At that time there was very little distinction between pedophiles and homosexuals. The comment that would come out every time is that they should be strung up by the balls and shot. I don't have objections to that, when it comes to pedophiles, quite frankly (ha, ha, ha). However, it was the connection. The distinction was not made then about the two, Gay/Pedophilia. So one wasn't obviously going to say too much and the conversation you heard, I mean, you just didn't. It wasn't something you were going to say anything about and in a small town because you only had to get on the wrong side of what was said and you never got moved back to the right side of that line in a small town. The only thing... I knew there was a lesbian couple in this area and certainly had seen one of the women, not the other. I knew whose sister she was and they were talked about in whispers, of course. So I wasn't saying anything to anyone down here. I just got into a relationship out of residence and certainly that person came back with me but nothing was said, as such. Now I don't know, my brother may have already known at that point. I'm not sure and I don't remember. My older brother... when that came about... but he certainly was aware. In fact it may have been my younger brother. He came to live with me in Montreal for awhile while I was living with Pinky.

When you were living with Pinky?

Yes.

Pinky, who was your lover?

Yes. Did I get totally side tracked on your question here?

No, no. So you didn't feel that you could come out to your family members, or your neighbors or people you had grown up with?

No, no. It would not have been a good thing to do. I knew in my mother's heart that she would not reject me. I knew that. I knew she wouldn't be happy; but she wouldn't reject me. My biggest fear was that I knew that it was something that my father would use to hurt my mother. He was such a cold, cruel man. He would use it on her. It would be her fault; she would be a lesbian; she would be out doing those things. So as much as anything, it was keeping fuel from the fire.

Your father would blame your mother and use it against her?

Oh yeah. Yes. Whatever he could use, he would use. Oh yeah.

Anything shameful?

It didn't have to be shameful. I mean… she had a dog and she loved the dog, so he choked the dog. He was that kind of a sort of a son of a bitch. He was just a very cruel man.

Oh, yeah, yeah.

Oh yeah. So if he could use that to hurt her well then he would.

Yes, so you knew that and so you kept it to yourself?

Yes. Yes.

Did you suffer any losses or were you celebrated in any way because of your lesbian identity?

Certainly not celebrated. Losses… yeah…I don't know about losses… but… I mean, I still have a friend here. We've been friends since 1956. So we've been friends for fifty-three or fifty-four years. Now, I haven't said anything to her, she's a smart woman, but she has to know. She's married to a red neck and I know it's easier for her not to have to defend anything. Like her comment one day is, we were talking about people telling you things, you know, sometimes that was good, sometimes it was bad, and she said to me, she looked at me and said, "And then there are these things that you really wish they wouldn't tell you." Now that said to me that if I didn't say anything to her, then she can go merrily along and she doesn't have to deal with any of that or anybody's comments. She can just say, "I don't know." So I thought, well if that's where she's comfortable – fine, you know. It doesn't matter to me but if she's comfortable, well that's o.k.. As far as anyone else? I don't talk to the rest of my family here. I'm not close to the rest of my family. I have a cousin out in Vancouver and he bought it up to me. He knew that I was gay. Somebody told him, but I don't know who. Probably the whole damn family knows. I don't know. The one time I did get into it with my father, because he did exactly what he said he wouldn't do, and he asked me one night. My mother had gone off to bed and he asked me if I was gay?

Your father?

Yes. I think I said, 'Well, why do you want to know? What the hell difference does it make to you?' He said ta-da-da-da-da-da-da-da and he just wanted to know because??? I told him that nobody has ever asked me that I had ever lied to them about it. If I avoided it in some cases then I have avoided it, but I have never lied about it. I'll tell you the truth on one condition. I mean, at this point, I was, I don't know, probably close to forty and I had refused to ask that man for anything since I was sixteen. It killed me to ask him for a quarter back then to visit a friend in the hospital who just had a baby. Anyway, that's another whole story. So I said, "If you promise to leave Mom out of this and to never bring it up to her then I will tell you the truth." "Oh, I promise," he said. So I said, "Yes, I am." The next day he was on to my mother about it. She was out there screwing around with all those women; just the two of us; ta-da-da-da-da-da-da-da. You know, I wasted my bloody time. It's the way he is.

Did you lose any jobs over the years, do you think?

No. No, because at the hospital there were a lot of gays at the hospital. Pshyc Hospital in Montreal there were a lot of gays there. There are probably a number of jobs they didn't know. I remember going in and seeing a doctor in Vancouver when I was running the women's shelter, you know, she was the same doctor that was serving the women's shelter. On something that I had gotten done she said, "I didn't know that you were gay." I said, 'Well, you didn't have a reason to know." She said, "Well, you're right." (ha, ha, ha). So I know I've been in situations and places where people didn't know or weren't sure because if anybody ever asked me I would tell them. So some jobs I was in for years and it simply never came up. Some situations where it might have come up after years and I said, "Well sorry it doesn't apply because I'm gay." There was nothing more about it. When I was at St. Catherine's working with kids, they all knew about it there because Kyra used to, we all used to go out as a group and Kyra was my partner at that time and she always came.

How do you spell that name?

Kyra... K –y – r – a.

So you don't feel it's affected your work life?

No. For the most part I don't because, like I said, all the years at the hospital everybody there knew I was gay. Now that's not to say there wasn't prejudice and there wasn't people that didn't give you a hard time about it because there certainly were. I mean you could walk into the cafeteria and have a whole table snickering away and you know what they were doing and saying or somebody made a comment. So it's not like it wasn't there. I certainly saw the prejudice. Did it affect me directly? I don't think a whole lot because, probably it's just not anything, and I can have a lot roll off my back and go ahead and say it if you have anything to say. I don't give a shit, you know. Oh you would never know that I did. So I don't think... now were it known when I was with the Salvation Army... I think... yeah... it might have made an effect there. Now that's not entirely true because some people did know but not very many. I certainly don't think the Captain and upwards knew. (Ha, ha, ha) I don't think so. I can't say anywhere else that it affected my work because I don't think it did.

How has the Church offered you pastoral care when you came to recognize your Lesbian Identity?

It was irrelevant, just irrelevant. There might have been a time... now I went through a period after I left here and was into a relationship with Pinky. She had a young son and I had a whole lot more living I wanted to do before I was ready to settle down because I was only nineteen. I was only eighteen when the relationship started... but that's all right too. What was I going to say? Oh... there was a period, also at that time, I don't know if you ran into it, but there was so much dysfunction in the gay community back then. Everybody was sort of coming out from the boondocks and there hadn't been a sense of community. It wasn't like it is today by any means. After I left here, I decided I wanted to move away from that. There was so much anger. A lot of these women were really hurting and they had so much anger. Almost every time you got together to have a good time, it ended up with someone fighting. I grew up with this fighting and battling at home and I didn't want to be a part of that. So I decided that... well...maybe I wasn't gay! I came up with this. Maybe I was so angry coming out of the situation that I had grown up with and the rest of the world wasn't like my father was. So maybe I should give the other side of the world a chance. This was my one swing of the pendulum back in the other direction... which didn't last terribly long. I had moved out and I didn't live with Pinky anymore. I was in my own apartment but we still got together, sort of thing, because she didn't want to break up. However, I had to look at this other side, sort of thing. Now... that may have been a time, had I been at all into religion, that I might have wanted to use the Church or some of it's services to help me look at that. However, it certainly wasn't something that I considered as an option.

Why? Did you feel they would reject you?

Well, I didn't think they had any relevance to me. I mean here I am the deviant. What is organized religion going to give to me? By this time, as well, there is no doubt I had already started to develop some very strong feelings about the Church and what I've seen. When I say the Church, I mean any organized Church religion. I was not very impressed with the results that were based on history. Where were all the wars? Where did they come out off? Basically they are all bloody religious wars. Go back to the Crusades. It is the Catholics against the Protestants, I mean, today it's... we know what's going on today. Religion has done more harm than good as far as I'm concerned. ... I think I'm going off on a tangent again... I think religion has some good tenets. There are some good principles; but I think that so many individuals have taken and bastardized everything so much that I just don't have much use for it. I think it does more harm than good.

So you wouldn't say it has helped you in any way during difficult times in your life then?

No. No.

What has been your experience of the Church's teachings in reference to human sexuality?

I have no personal experience in that I haven't gone into a Church for many, many years. I'm one of these people who I don't know if I'm going to be up all night or wake up four in the morning. I only get three channels, so what do I get first thing in the morning? You know what I get. At five in the morning I'm going to get the Evangelist Song there; I'm going to get the Faith Healers on the T.V. I'm going to get a lot of time of Jerry Farwell. I listen to a lot of those people. They're not doing me any favors and I don't think they are doing anybody else any favors. So, my experience basically with the Church, since the time I was a teenager and no longer whipped, has been what I've seen on the T.V., read in the newspaper, watched on the news, or discussions and debates and I am not impressed.

Do you feel their teaching untruths about homosexuals?

There are certainly...I mean there are so many factions out there that... yes... some of them, as far as I'm concerned, is... absolutely untruths. There's no doubt in my mind about it and yes, they are out there teaching it to their heart's content. There are lots who don't though. But for the most part, to this day, even with some of the changes that have occurred, in my book, even if I were a believer, I wouldn't feel Church was a very welcoming place.

For a gay person?

Yes, absolutely.

So you haven't taken a partner to Church and felt comfortable?

No. No and nor have I gone to Church with a partner, and I have had partners who have gone to Church, but I have no desire to go to Church.

How do you experience your relationship with the Church at the present time?

It's an interesting phenomenon that when you strike a certain age, and we know that there's an awful lot of people who hit that certain age, and get religion. I've looked at that, over the years, and tried to analyze what's happening there. I think I can, to a great extent, understand what happens to a lot of people with age, younger as well. I mean there have certainly been times in my life where I have really envied my friends that have religion; that have God, because they can always go and they have, and believe they have, a support, a strength, somewhere to turn to. I can be envious of that. I can be jealous of that. I can wish, 'Gee, I wish I had that because I could really use that kind of support right now.' But based on what? It would have to be based on a belief in God. I don't believe in God.

So you have no relationship with the Church at the present time?

No, none. Having looked at it and having thought 'Gee, it would be nice' However, you can't just jump into it saying, 'Here I am.' It sure as hell doesn't work for me.

Do you feel that the Church has kept you from having a relationship with God, with their attitudes towards gay people?

Well, you're asking me if one thing has kept me from having a belief than another. I can't say that one... that the Church has done it. No, I wouldn't say it was the Church but life has done it. I grew up and every Sunday we went to my grandmother's. Every Sunday they drove Jordy up to Gospel Hall. Every Sunday there was nothing on that Radio, it was times before T.V., but it was religious programs. I can sing you every old hymn there was because I listened to them every Sunday of my life growing up. But I don't, I saw too much crap to believe that there's a good entity called God that allows us to go on. I couldn't believe in him. Religion tells us that God is good. Then there's always crap in life. I can't believe because my reality is this – in my mind, no good God is going to allow this to happen. It wasn't just, you know, I had a pretty shitty life; but there were good parts too. I have also worked with a lot of kids that have had really crappy lives and a lot of adults that have had really crappy lives. I probably know more than an awful lot of people just how much evil there is in this world. So I can't see this and believe God exists.

You can't reconcile evil with a good God?

Right.

So that has nothing to do with your lesbian Identity? It's just your life experience?

Yes, but the lesbian identity would come into it since that's part of who I am. So maybe if at ten or eleven when I was first having my first obviously lesbian thoughts that I could have been able to say something in that C.G.I.T. Meeting… or in that… you know…

The C.G.I.T. Youth Group?

Yeah. Well, then maybe, I would have felt different but I sure didn't feel that I had a forum to say anything.

You didn't feel your questions would have been welcome there?

No, absolutely not. Absolutely not.

So, is there anything you would like to say to the Church in reference to your lesbian identity?

That's not one that I would like to answer right off the top of my head. That's one that if I were going to answer then I would really like some time to think on it.

How about I go to the washroom? (ha, ha, ha)

You think that's going to be enough time!

Is that going to be enough time?

No. That's not going to be enough time. No.

Could you just give some, off the top of your head, some comments?

Read your question again and I'll try to.

Is there anything you would like to say to the Church in reference to your Lesbian Identity?

Off the top of my head! My lesbian identity is part of who I am. Part of who I am. As a concern particularly for younger gays and lesbians that are still growing up in small towns, in small communities often with small minds. These kids are afraid and they don't know what the hell's happening to themselves many times but they know what it's like being in a school and somebody calling the guy down the hall a fag or being in a group and somebody doing something similar. I don't think these kids, when they really need it, and need the kind of support that says it's all right to question yourself and wonder who you are. I don't think the Church, to this day, gives the kids the opportunity to do that. I think, basically, they are still being told that it's wrong. I think it's the worst thing that we are doing. We are still doing this to the kids and kids are still committing suicide.

Kids are still committing suicide over this?

You bet they are. You bet you. They're still afraid. They're still being told by organized Religion that it's wrong, it's evil, or even if it's not the act is. But let's face it hormones at this age are raging. Kids are up and down like bouncing balls and they are confused enough without having to try and make that sort of distinction. They just need support at that age. To be told that it's all right to be who they are and to take the time to find out, but not to be rejected. They should not feel that their only way out is the long way out. It happens way too often.

And you feel the Church has a responsibility in this area?

I absolutely do…yes. Again, if you look back, where does the anti gay sentiment come from? The Church, that's were it comes from. Pulled right out of the good old little Bible is that one nice little quote. That's all you need for most people. One can stand up and give you a three hour sermon on one little line. So no…I do believe the Church does have a responsibility there; and I do believe they could be doing a whole lot more to help the kids. That… that I do. So, that's off the top of my head. Is that enough for you?

Yes…Thanks… Thank-you.

Are we done?

Yes… Yes, thanks… Thank-you very much.

Joy's Tape

What has been your connection with the Church?

Well my connection with the Church has been all my life. From the time I was a baby and I was christened in this Church, which is across the road there. So, it's a long connection since I'm now fifty-four. Now, I went to Church as a child and to Sunday school and I joined the Church. I remember when I joined the Church that my father was an Elder and when he shook my hand at the end of the thing, he squeezed my hand. But, I actually remember feeling rather doubtful about whether I really believed at that time because of my...... but anyway.

I spent some time in Britain. When I was in Britain, I didn't find a Church that I related to as well as the United Church. I didn't know the hymns. I occasionally went to different Anglican Churches. They were very high Anglicans. So they were rather foreign too, being with the incenses and all the different things; the marching in; it did seem a little more ceremony; a little more pompous; to me a lot more stained glass. It was rather unfamiliar. Maybe at Christmas time or sometimes I would go. One time I heard Desmond Tutu speak in England in one of the Anglican Churches. On the other hand, I didn't find...there was just no United. There's nothing like the United Church. The United Church, I think, is just such a progressive Church. There's nothing like that, and there's something about not knowing the hymns. I love to sing and when you don't know the hymns, it's hard to relate. Friends of mine were Baptist and they were very involved in this Baptist Church. A very fundamentalist group; but that didn't turn my crank. So I guess I was away from the Church for a number of years really. When I lived in Halifax, I guess I went to the United Church there some. I did a youth group there. But, moving back to back home ten years ago, I found it a solace to go back to the Church, and to be part of the community which was not just the Church community; but my village community. Oh and to be known. It was important for me to be among people that knew me and knew who I was. So there is a lot of fellowship that I felt by returning back to the Church. I am an occasional attendee now, but I also do help out with functions, Church suppers and so forth if we can…and that's it, that's it.

How would you describe your awakening to your lesbian identity?

I like the way that's phrased "awakening". I would describe my awakening to my identity as gradual. It was a political process almost. It was because I was in a group of a consciousness kind of raising group, which was an accountability group, and I learned about assertiveness. I became an assertiveness Teacher. I became well angry and bitter towards my husband, whom I felt was not doing his share. So that was how I started to become a lesbian. I just became more fed up with men really and became more and more so. So I left my husband and even though I initially was still going out with men, I did challenge the idea that, you know, that I supported lesbians. So it became a consciousness-raising thing. There were a lot of feminists around, and as I became a feminist, I became increasingly dis-enamoured with the neutral family of man in it, and that's just how it happened. So I started going out with women. Once I started going out with women it was just so much nicer that I wouldn't ever go back now.

Were you able to share this identity with the people closest to you?

I think I felt quite…oh…I wanted to hide it, initially. I remember one time when my mother and my aunt were over in Great Britain, and I was actually in the midst of breaking up with a woman and she threatened to "out" me and I didn't feel it was the right time. It was about 1988 and I wasn't ready to be "outed". In fact, my mother "outed" me. Well, I guess she realized that there wasn't a guy around for awhile. We were out in the garden picking raspberries one summer when I was home and she said to me, "Oh Joy", she said, "sometimes I think you must be lesbian." Then I said, "yes, you're right, I am." So that is how it came about that I was "outed". So my mother was very aware of what was going on more than I had expected her to be. I will tell you that her next line was, "it is not what God wants." I think I said, "I didn't know you had a direct line to God".!

Did you suffer any losses or were you celebrated in any way because of your lesbian identity?

It's a very interesting turn of phrase. No, I wouldn't say it was celebrated. Like I said, my mother said to me that it wasn't God's will and that she was ashamed of me and that my father would be ashamed of me and that he would turn over in his grave and da-te-da-te-da-te-da. I have experienced a fair amount of rejection from my family over it. Initially, my sister and brother-in-law, they were very opposed and very guilting me about my daughter and what a hard thing it was for her, etc., etc., and my brother. I think there is still a fair share of alienation from my brother. I would say that my mother has done not too badly but she... she sometimes is negative towards Marie. She blames Marie, "Well Marie, she did it, you know." This is very unfair as Marie does a lot for her. And she is very quick to condemn and blame. But she hasn't done too badly considering her age and accepting our life style. But she can easily be manipulated too. She says what people want to hear sometimes. So the answer is -Yes, I have experienced quite a bit of loss in becoming a lesbian. I think from my family more than my work contacts and strangers and people I've met subsequently. I think that the most rejection has been from my family. The most hurt.

How has the Church offered you pastoral care as you came to recognize your lesbian identity?

Well, the time I became to recognize my lesbian identity, I was not really a part of the Church congregation because as I said I was living in Britain and I didn't really find a Church that I was really that happy with. So I didn't. It was really irrelevant to me then; and I guess I was more of an Agnostic at that time. I was living in Britain and I was very socialist minded. I don't think I found God all that relevant...to fast forward to living here in particular, when I first came back to here, I came with a partner and in that first year it was very rough for us and we didn't have a lot of money, and we moved and we were caring for my daughter, and still we broke up. I found a lot of solace in the Church, in returning to the Church.

How has the Church offered you pastoral care as you came to recognize your lesbian identity?

As I said, as I became to recognize it, it was a different situation at the time and it was not relevant at the time. As I maintained and developed my lesbian relationship was the Church helpful? Well, as I told you the story, I remember feeling a very, very depressed and groundless and not really having many friends when I first returned back to Canada in 1988. I had broken up from my partner and moved back to this house. That was the winter the year Mom was living in Florida. I was pretty sad and pretty depressed, and I did find a lot of acceptance and a lot of solace in just going to the Church, and being among many people who knew me. So there was a lot of acceptance there. I found that very helpful.

So the Church was very helpful at that time?

Yes, at that time. When I was faced with….I was very depressed. I was faced with a very difficult break up.

Did they know that it was a Lesbian break up?

It's a pretty small community. I would be very surprised if they didn't.

And so during painful times, like a break up, the Church was helpful?

Yes. I found it helpful. I didn't know if I had gone anywhere else it would have been the same; but what was most helpful for me was to be among people that I had known all of my life. For them to see me and recognize me and be happy to see me at Church. It was like the sense of community I felt was healing.

The community was healing?

Yes. The sense of community that I felt, you know.

Has the Church offered you pastoral care in dealing with the hatred of others? Have you experienced Homophobia?

I can't really say I have experienced a lot of homophobia personally. Except for the rejection of my family. I don't know. I think I protected myself from not necessarily coming out. Of course, there has been a recent incident in our Church where two members, in fact the Organist and the Chair of the Board of Stewards, very influential members of the Church, decided to leave the Church because they took exception to the publicity that was done by another fellow Church in a leaflet to tell lesbian and gay teenagers where to find help if they were ever confused about their sexuality. So this member of our congregation decided to leave the Church because he didn't agree with it. He felt it was promoting or recruiting lesbians and gays…which was totally ridiculous. Anyway, he took exception and decided to leave the Church and when I found out about it, I was actually away when it all came to a head, I actually cried. I felt so sad and so upset I cried. This was a neighbor of mine and someone I knew all my life, who feels like that, and so I really felt I should talk to him and yet I never seem to find the opportunity. However, I did write the Presbytery about my views and, you know, what a tragedy I felt when good people choose it in their hearts to hate and fear others. Anyway, that's what I said. But I only got to talk to him on the phone; unfortunately, I think it would have been better person to person if I had talked to him and his wife. They accused me of not really taking much notice of the Bible and didn't the Bible mean anything to me? They felt…I asked them why they hated me so much and they told me they didn't. I realized after that it wasn't hatred that was there but the fear. The fear is pretty deep. They say that their children are coming of an age where they will become sexually active and that they don't want them to be… something like this. This could influence them in a wrong direction. I told them that I felt that when their children were of legal age and they were going to be sexually active, it would be nothing they could do about it. It would be their choice; but it was just not their children… but their grandchildren that they feared about. And I just find that so sad. It was a very evident homophobia. And at that time it was a lot of hoop-la and a lot of questions were raised. These people chose to join the Presbyterian Church, and the woman chose to leave the choir. As the Choir Director after many years and she was very good at it. So it was rather sad. But I did have to acknowledge that the Minister here, at the time, was excellent in challenging it. He said that the United Church was not the Church for the upper and middle classes; but a Church for everyone, and we can't back down on this, and this is very important. He was very powerful in challenging the man and I really respected and thanked him for it. So in that way, and I don't know how every Minister would have responded. I don't know but I think it took a lot of guts for him to do that and he was a fine example. He is now left though, which is interesting, which may have precipitated his departure, but he did have to…it was hard, very hard for him and I did thank him.

What has been your experience of the Church's teachings in reference to human sexuality?

I really can't say that in growing up that I've been aware of any teachings of the Church. Oh, I do remember when I was probably a bit of an unruly teenager that this man, who always had a bright red face, he was a farmer and very salt of the earth, and he was our Sunday School Teacher and Superintendent of the older kids. I remember challenging him of the virgin birth and I remember him going scarlet red. So…that was…oh dear…I guess that was part of it. What else?…. what else?…Oh, I know when the story of Ruth and Naomi was read the other Sunday in Church, oh it must have been in the Spring or sometime, I was nodding and winking at Marie…" See, see they were lesbians… 'whither thou goest, I will go'". I know that's one of the ones that lesbians like to claim as their own. And Jonathan, wasn't Jonathan suppose to be gay? It says quite clearly in the Bible that he was gay. But, I'm not familiar enough with the Scriptures to know.

But I do know, as I said already, that the United Church's stand is very aggressive and that our local Minister has stood up, and our progressive stance of the United Church has accepted and supported it, despite the controversy and the uproar that it caused. And I do feel that there is a role here in educating the masses here. We should have discussion groups on sexuality of lesbian and gays and the Church, sometime down the road. It is not a good time to do it when it is too heated. Like what does homophobia look like? Like what does that mean? What are some of the things that we have to do to protect ourselves from? Even in little ways, like with clients that I don't know when talking about my partner? I find different ways of phrasing sentences so that I don't say he or she with people when I'm working. I'm full out with a lot of people at work, but you know, how you find, well they...we can find ways of talking about a person, your significant other, without being clear what gender they are. Just little ways like that that we protect us, or that I protect myself I should say to clarify.

Do you take your partner to Church?

Yes, in fact Marie and I sit in the front pew often. Yes, Marie and I often go to Church together and we are a lesbian couple there. People are friendly to us there and they know we are good workers and yes we feel happy being in Church.... Although I can tell you a funny story... We have sometimes, when the Minister is away on holidays or on a conference, we get a Lay Preacher. One of the Lay Preachers we got was this guy who is very involved with the Bible School, and he is Salvation Army, and very opposed to the gays and lesbians. He has actually been accused; he is a Principal at a school, of taking the boys aside and telling them not to be gay in his school, some time ago. He is Marie's Principal and also a Lay Preacher for the Bible Society. On this particular Sunday morning, he comes bouncing up to the pulpit and looks down. The two people in the front pew, with my mother, are me and Marie. Well, it was obvious; it was so funny because he obviously was so stunned that he had to do a double take. It took him two minutes before he could open his mouth and say anything, and try to get his breath. He was so surprised to see us. His teacher that he works with all week, sitting in the front pew, when he has gone all way out in the woods to make a little sermon. So, it was quite funny really. He's always friendly to us, though, and he always puts on a front and is friendly to us. I just thought that you would like to know that little story.

How do you experience your relationship with the Church at the present time?

Well, I consider myself as a member of the United Church. That's where I joined the Church and where I never changed my membership. That's where I was baptized, so I consider the Church down the road as my Church. I speak of it as my Church. Not that I'm that involved in any of the activities there on a regular basis, but as an occasional Church goer. At one point, Marie and I made a bargain with each other, that she would take Mom one Sunday and I would take her the next Sunday, which is a little bit unfair really. And of course we would go for holidays. We're sort of a holiday Church goers, but it really depends on what's on...I might be away or whatever. So, I'm really a casual attendee; but I consider myself a member and I love the Church. I love the way it looks and I love everything about it and I know the people there. My intentions are, when I have a little more time and I retire, to become better at doing something. I really think I would like to have some kind of a youth group...either Explorers or CGIT or something like that, or Sunday School. I do plan to give something, a little bit, back. I must say that was one of the things that my Church really enriched my life as a child growing up. I always attended the Church groups. There was always a Church group. Explorers and CGIT and I always went to CGIT camp. I used to go to camp every summer and I never missed it. That was a rich blessing for me to have, that something outside the family... that social atmosphere. So, I felt blessed to have such a Church in my environment. Oh, and such a beautiful building, such a beautiful situation being right on the river. I do look at it with love. I do look at that Church with love and care and concern. I want it to prosper and flourish and I must say that my friends that are United

Church members down in Halifax were part of the Board of Stewards, and they used to have this thing, where they would get people who, even if they missed Sunday, would get them to put their collections in for every week. So now, I'm kind of mindful of this and if I miss a few Sundays, then I try and put a $20 in the plate instead. And I have envelopes, so I must be a member, and I do put a little more in the envelopes if I miss a few Sundays, in order to try and make up. So I do feel committed to it, and I feel it's my Church and I love it. As I said, I love its beauty.

And not only that, I must say, I loved our previous Minister. He was just perfect for me. I just loved his messages and they were always good. It was always, I guess, I have been talking about the physical and the community; but there is a sense when it is very important to have a Spiritual Leader. I must say that our past Minister was just that. I saw, as a Spiritual Leader, that he always had a very important thing to tell us or to talk that were topical. His sermons were good. They made you think, and it made you question, and it made you believe… you know…and that's also what I look for in the Church's spiritual nurturing, I guess.

Is there anything you would like to say to the Church in reference to your lesbian identity?

The first thing I could think about is the trite little thing that we say on the Gay Pride Marches, "we're here, and we're Queer, so get used to it". "We're here, and we're Queer, so get over it." Or something like that. Well, I guess it's like not that safe a place to be. I mean, knowing a few lesbian Ministers, I feel rather sad about how unsafe they experience it to be. They are loved and they preach good sermons, and everyone likes them, and they lead youth groups, and they do wonderful things; but yet, they're terrified to "come out". They're terrified…even if everyone seems to know, but they're still terrified. I think that's really tragic. If it isn't safe to be "out" in the United Church, well where would it ever be safe to be "out"? I just think that that's so tragic. So, that's what I would like to say. I don't know, I guess Wanda's point was that she did "come out" once and it wasn't worth her while to live there anymore. They made life so difficult for her that she left. So, I don't know, that is something I would like to say to the Church is that - think carefully and look at…I don't know…it's such a tremendous job. I don't know how you can do that. How the Church, the general body, could do that. At one point, when this incident happened in the fall, I was so keen. I was really, really committed to do some consciousness raising of the Church. I was thinking of getting some program together and do some training. This could be my new career. I really could envision really doing some important and interesting consciousness raising amongst the different congregations. But that was a pipe dream, I guess. But that's one thing I would like to do though, really. It would be fascinating. So, yes. On the other hand, the United Church has done so much for most people, I have felt in therapy that I've slashed my way through bushes and jungle and high grass and struggled…and struggled…and only to reach the foot of the mountain…you know… and that's what it must feel like to the powers of be and how hard it is to change people's minds. But I think they've done well, but it's a long way to go.

Mary's Tape

What has been your connection with the Church?

I was bought up Catholic. As a Catholic, I went to Church almost every Sunday. I received all the Sacraments throughout my childhood, attended Mass faithfully, because you had to... every Sunday you went to Church... a Catholic Church. Quite regularly I went to Church because, you know, I found I enjoyed it. I became a big part of the Church. I was on the Parish Council; I was the Chair of the Parish Council of my Church; I was... I did the Readings; I organized the Readings... the Lecturers in my Church for the Readings. I was also a Sponsor for people joining the Church like at Easter you join the Church. So I was a Sponsor for and in a... I organized a process for people joining the Church at Easter time. I took different courses from Sisters in the area on religious themes. I was there to decorate the Church when it was Christmas time, or Easter time, so I was, you know, very involved. I think, later on in life, still being involved in the Church that I still didn't have peace. It didn't matter... go to Church, not go to Church or anything, I just didn't have an inner peace. So when I met my partner and she lived outside of my area and she also had connections to a different Church, the United Church, I stopped going to the Catholic Church - on a regular basis. I did go back at times. I still go back like at Lent I'll go back and I will go into the area and I will light a candle. Like when my Aunt had surgery this summer, I went to the Church and I prayed and I lit a candle for her. At other times when I feel in need, I will go sit in the Catholic Church and I'll light a candle and I will pray to the Creator, to whomever, and I find it peaceful. But now I go to the United Church here in.

So your life in the Church, previous to this, it was having to do with kind of functions - functioning, decorating, finding lecturers. It was kind of a doing thing?

Yes, right.

So you found that your faith life was nurtured in another denomination; in the United Church?

Yes, right. In the United Church., yeah right because as a lesbian the United Church is more open to lesbians. It is more accepting. It's all the same God except they understand God in a different way than the Catholics and they accept lesbians whereas the Catholics and the Catholic faith - they don't.

And so that was the reason why you didn't have peace. You didn't feel accepted?

No. Peace was a lot of things to do with my personal life besides the Church life.

So did it bother you for all those years that they didn't accept gay people…lesbian people?

No. Because I didn't consider myself gay all those years - or lesbian… right?

Oh, I see

Yes right. I came through the Catholic Church as a child, as a teenager, as a young adult and didn't recognize myself as being gay or lesbian.

So when you did?

When I accepted the fact that I was a lesbian, then my thoughts were, you know, oh you can't be Catholic and be a lesbian. They just don't accept it.

So, you had a crisis then…faith in a way?

Yeah.

Ok.

There was one Sister Millie and her family went to a Catholic Church and she did courses and she did the course where I sponsored someone to join the Church at Easter. So, you know, we became friends in a way. And I think I would have liked to have joined the Church. I should have joined the Church, the United Church here at Easter when David was here because I liked him as a Minister and I just never thought of it.

So you are quite committed to the Church?

Yes. I miss not being a Lecturer, you know, like when they do those readings on Sunday. I know them. I know them better than other people I know...right? 'Cause I 've done them... right?

So you would like to do that?

Oh yes and I was good at it...right? And I enjoyed doing that.

Yeah...So you feel that's a ministry that you're missing right now?

Yeah. Since I'm not part of this Church, I'm not a member of this Church. Like I do service work. I help out at different functions they have, but I don't take part in the service.

Yeah.

Yeah.

But you could?

I think I have to become a member first.

Before you could be a lecturer?

Don't you?

No. Not necessarily. No.

What would the congregation think if you got up there, started reading, and you're not even a member of the Church?

Oh, I think in the United Church anyone who would like to do that kind of work is welcome to do it.

That's your personal opinion.

No...Well in our Church it's that way.

Oh!!

Yeah.

Well, read the next question.

How would you describe your awakening to your lesbian identity?

My awakening...as my friend said, she knew I was lesbian before I did. And it's true in a lot of cases. Personally, my awakening was someone else became attracted to me and sort of wanted me and therefore became attached to me and became part of my life. Therefore, it sort of developed from a friendship and I did have some awareness that I was a lesbian; but I wasn't going out to do anything about it. This other person did something about it for me.

And was that shocking to you or did it seem natural?

No. It seemed natural. It just seemed to flow and that was it. No, it wasn't a shock because this other friend that said, "I knew you were lesbian before you did,"... like she and I would talk because she was open. Lesbian in her work, everywhere like, and like we were good friends, and we would have conversations about, you know, lesbians, relationships, and things. So it wasn't new at that time. So, no it wasn't a shock.

So, it was a gradual awakening in a way?

Yes…gradual.

Ok. Not terribly traumatic, just gradual.

Yes, just gradual. No it wasn't traumatic.

And a feeling of naturalism?

Yes.

Ok., Thank-you.

Were you able to share this identity with the people closest to you?

Well, I didn't come out and just tell people because I think people knew. And the people that were closest to me would be my family. So, I didn't hide anything. We became partners, we went places, and we did things together. So… But I just didn't come out and say I was a lesbian now… right? And my family accepted it and, if anybody, I was the one that held back and wouldn't do things with the family cause none of them did anything against it… you know… so…

They didn't seem to have a problem with it?

No.

But you had a problem sharing that with them?

Yeah. I would say I didn't go visiting them as much after that.

Why? Because you felt they would exclude you?

No. Because its almost, in a way, I excluded myself.

You excluded yourself?

Yeah.

You felt you didn't belong in a way?

No. I felt I didn't want…in case they didn't accept it. I didn't want to be there for them to have to tell.

Oh, I see.

Right… if I wasn't there?

Well, if you weren't there, they couldn't reject you.

Yes, right.

I see. So you anticipated some rejection?

Yes. Being from a Catholic background family, you know, the religion itself would make them.

Yes. So you thought that following their religion, they would reject you?

Right. But as I see it now, the religion background might reject me, but person wise they don't reject me at all.

No….and never had?

No, that was my issue, not theirs because they accept me and I see that now.

How did you get the message that you were accepted, after awhile?

Because when I did go to visit them, nothing had changed. They were still the same. They talked to me; they were still friendly, you know; they treated me the same way. They treated my partner with respect and with, you know, friendliness, and acceptance, and didn't show any sign of rejecting us and we became a part of the event that we went to. They showed acceptance.

And it remained that way?

Yeah.

Did you suffer any losses or were you celebrated in any way because of your lesbian identity?

At this moment, I can't think of any losses. The celebration would be of the community of lesbians that accepted me and welcomed me and whom became my friends. That would be a celebration.

And so, you had no losses that you feel?

That I feel…No.

How has the Church offered you pastoral care in the following?

- As you came to recognize your lesbian identity?

As I came to recognize being a lesbian, the Church didn't know I was and I didn't tell them. So, they wouldn't have that knowledge. So they neither helped nor hindered it. But the hindrance was that it was a Catholic Church and their policy on lesbianism is very well known. The hindrance was that I, as a lesbian, would not be accepted in the Catholic Church and practice being a lesbian at the same time. So, therefore, I was the one who cut my ties with the Church.

Did you have a fear of discovery?

In the Church?

Yes.

Yes, in a way, yes. Because sometimes I would go to Mass, and I would go to Communion and the thought would be there sometimes, you know, 'what would they say?' However I still went and I still go... right.

Has the Church offered you pastoral care as you developed and maintained your lesbian relationship?

As I developed and maintained my lesbian relationships, I no longer went to the Catholic Church on a regular basis. I went to the United Church and found the minister there and the congregation accepted us as being part of their services.

So, you felt you could be open about who you were?

Yes, in the United Church, yes. Because it was in the community in which we lived and people who went to Church knew...right?

And has the Church offered you pastoral care during times of death and illness?

I still had connections to the Catholic Church when my father died and I knew the priest well, Father was very helpful at that time when Dad died and he did the service for us and the funeral and he was very helpful.

Did he know you were a lesbian?

He would have known at that time. Yes, because I was there with my partner.

Oh, yes. And he treated your partner with respect?

Oh, yes.

Did you ever have to deal with the hatred of others, and if so, has the Church offered you pastoral care?

I haven't had to deal with that.

You didn't have to deal with that?

No.

Nothing at work? Nothing in the community?

No.

Ok. What has been your experience of the Church's teachings in reference to human sexuality?

The Catholic Church's teachings are based on mother, father, children, and family model. Whereas the father is the bread winner of the family, the mother is the housekeeper and looked after it, and the kids look up to them and they go to school and they are obedient and well behaved. Modern, or up-to-date, United Church ministry and sermons is more acceptant of different types of families. When he preached he talks about families that are different and don't have a mother and a father. They have…some families only have one parent, some families children are bought up by grandparents. They also accept same-sex couples as being a family. So there's just different make-ups, groups that make up families.

So when you were growing up, there was one model?

Yes, one model. mother, father, kids - that was your model.

Ok. Have you felt free to take your partner to Church or do you feel you must hide your relationship?

I feel free to take my partner to Church. We go to a United Church in our community in which we live. We are well accepted in the Church as part of the Church community and the Church family.

How do you experience your relationship with the Church at the present time?

At the present time, I go to the United Church ; but not every Sunday. I am not a member of the Church. I haven't joined the Church yet, but I am more comfortable with the idea of joining in the United Church because of it's teachings and its philosophy. And it's something I likely will do in the future.

Is there anything you would like to say to the Church in reference to your lesbian identity?

Being a lesbian, doesn't make me worship any different than anybody else. I can still worship; I still can pray; I can be a part of the community. It makes no difference if I am a lesbian or not a lesbian…I'm a member of the Church… and I participate.

Do you have all the rights and privileges of all the people in the Church? For example: Marriage?

No. Lesbians don't have the privilege of being married.

Is that hurtful?

Well this summer we got the closest you can get to being married. We got a Registered Domestic Partnership, which legally gives us the rights of a couple; but it doesn't recognize you as marriage in the Church does. I think it's going to come. It's not that far off before we will have the right to marry. It's going to be legislated.

So you feel that it's coming and you feel no bitterness?

No. Then we have the rights the same as everybody else. Like, you know, a man and a woman - they can chose to marry or not to marry, or live common law or whatever type of relationship they want to have at that time. And we're denied that now because we can't get married and I think, not very far down the road, we will be able to get married and, therefore, then we have the opportunity of having that choice and like some people will choose to get married and some people won't.

So you would say to the Church that it is important that they allow lesbian people to marry in the Church?

Yes. It's important that lesbian and gays can marry in the Church. Then it puts them with heterosexual couples so that we have equality.

Do you think equality is an important virtue or value in the Church?

Equality is an important virtue everywhere…like people should be treated.

Equally?

As equally…yes.

In the Church, especially, would you say?

In the Church and in the community.

So would you say that the Church, by denying lesbians and gays the right to marry, is in a state of sin, if you will… in that it is saying that heterosexuals are first class citizens and homosexuals are second class citizens?

Well, yes they are distinguishing because we are not allowed to get married, and we are not recognized for that service. But I don't think that the Church can just say that we are going to allow this. It's coming from the government as our constitutional rights that we will be allowed to get married. The same as we are allowed to get benefits; we are allowed to have pensions. All of these things have taken place over the last couple of years and marriage is just the next thing that's going to happen. Once it's past then the Churches will have to put it in place because it will be allowed.

Is there a sacred dimension to marriage for You? Or is it just a legal understanding?

I have the legal understanding now. But the Church is sacred… right? It adds that to it.

So the sacred dimension is important to you?

Oh, yes. Yes, indeed.

And you feel the Church doesn't have the right to deny that to you?

Once the Law is passed, No.

You think it does now, even without waiting for the Government?

It has that right.

Does it have the right to say your relationship is not sacred?

I don't know if you can call it a right or not, but they do it. Just like they say women cannot be priests…right? soooooo - can't be done and that's it. It's their law.

Their law?

Yes.

What's to stop them from saying-well, that's a secular law if they pass the laws to marry gay people, but the Church has its own laws and we won't marry gay people.?

What happens then?

Yes.

That's when your majorities of people that agree that it can be done, step in and do something and it gets changed.

Well women have been kept out of the priesthood. We women have all kinds of rights in the secular society, but the Church has kept women away from the priesthood for centuries. What's to keep them from keeping Gay people from being married?

The Catholic Church?

Any Church. Can the Church decide for itself or does it have to follow the law?

It depends. I'm not a lawyer, so I don't know.

I mean the assumption that when the Government passes the law the Church will naturally follow?

But there are seventy-seven Churches. If this one won't marry you, then this one will. You just move Churches. All those Catholic lesbians and gays will just move to the United and get married… and say "the heck with you", and not give their money to the Catholic Church anymore… right?…so… All the Churches aren't going to say "No". The United Church is this much closer than the Catholic Church… right? So when the law comes they do the marriages and the people become United. Most of the people that join Churches anyway, only go to marriages, funerals and that's it. They never see them in the door again.

Yeah. (Shared Laughter)

Cause they go to Church twice a year, if they're lucky. So if they want a Church wedding, they just go and get married. That's what a lot of heterosexual people do now. You don't see a lot of those couples in your Church, once you marry them. If they want a Church to get married, they'll find a Church and get married.

So you figure it will be kind of like a patch work deal?

Patch work? In what way?

Well, that the whole body of Christ, the Church universal, won't embrace lesbian and gay marriages?

The whole Church as it is doesn't embrace everything now. The Catholic Church has these traditions and things and they haven't changed them. That's why all these Churches broke from the Catholic Church, because they didn't want to do it that way…right?… All these Churches came from the Catholic Church. You can go to the United Church and say, well they took that from the Mass… they took that from the Mass… they took that from the Mass… right?…They took what they wanted and left what they didn't. It's the same thing going to happen here. You don't want us to do it…we will go some place else that does it…right?

So you are following personal conscience rather than the authority of the Church?

But every Church has a different authority. There are women ministers… right? What authority have you… and what authority is the Catholic Church?… right? Their sticking to their authority

Well according to the Catholic understanding, they are the real authority, the real Church, and the rest are…?

But has that stopped everybody else from their religion? No. The Catholics are still there. They still have their Pope; they still have all these priests; they still have all these people that are Catholics. Then the other people who don't want them, they have their religion. So this authority that you are talking about, it isn't there anyway…right? Here are the Catholics and here's everybody else over here.

Jeanine's Tape

What has been your connection with the Church?

Since childhood?

Yes.

Well, even before I can remember, I know there are pictures of me being Christened or Baptized. So there's that kind of memory that is evoked from the pictures, and the certificate. I do have my Birth Certificate or Baptismal Certificate is what I should say. So there's that connection that I'm not aware of other than the pictures. After that, I know I was taken to Church regularly by my mother.

What denomination was this?

I was United, First United Church. My parents were from… they went to the First United Church and they were married there as well. When my father joined the Navy, we all moved to Dartmouth. We joined the First United Church. So, I was taken there as a child. I went to Sunday school; I was in the junior choir, the regular choir, so I was singing. I went to Explorers in that Church and certainly Sunday School. So there was a strong foundation being formed between myself and the United Church. So….

And then when you got married?

Right… I thought I was doing the right thing when my future mother-in-law approached me and said, "My son, my family, are Catholic and I will arrange for you to attend the R.C.I.A., the Rites for Catholic Initiation for Adults." It was very romantic to me, the notion of being, sort of, christened as a conscious adult making the decision to go forward into Catholicism. I felt a little bad about leaving the United Church; but I didn't articulate it that well because it just seemed that something bigger and better was waiting in Catholicism. After all, I was marrying into the Catholic kind of family. I was becoming all kinds of things; a wife, a daughter-in-law, and now I was going to become Catholic. So I had to go to the First United Church and get all kinds of Certificates and so on to bring to the Priest. I remember that it was a funny time going to this little office in the First United Church and asking for these forms and telling why I had to do that. So it pulled me a little bit; but still I was sort of pie eyed with the notion of becoming this wife, this daughter-in-law. The dutiful, do the right thing, and I gave absolutely no thought to what my parents would have thought. I wanted to be the good daughter to them too; but at the time it just seemed more important, that this put in front of me, I would become Catholic.

Ok, is there anything else you would like to say about that, your connection with the Church? Were you well received by the Catholic Church?

I was well received by the Catholic Church on the night that I became Catholic. This night… it was an Evening Mass and there were a lot of elderly people there, especially women. They were doing the Rosaries. They wept when I was called to the front of the Church. They cried… and after the service they came up to me and were saying prayers. It was very exotic to me. It was alien to anything I ever experienced in the United Church. So I felt as though I was a part of that. I became a Catechist. I taught for six years for the Lord's Church. At one point, I was teaching Catechists in how to be catechized. Then when I became divorced, I haven't been back to the Catholic Church since. Nobody has sought me out from either Church to see how I'm doing. So I don't feel a member of either Church at this point.

So were you a part of the Women's Society as well?

Yes, I did the turkey dinners and I was in the C.W.L. That was quite normal for me to experience because of my mother. I grew up with my mother doing the United Church Women, the U.C.W. stuff; the turkey dinners, the calling to make sure so and so bought the peas; and all of that. So it was just a normal part of it.

You have two children, is that correct?

Right.

Were they bought up in the Church?

Yes, they were.

So you had them Baptized and they were bought up with you?

Yes, I bought them up as Catholic. I had the romantic notion that my once husband would come to Church with us; but he only attended Church once in seventeen years with us. So he was absent from Church; but yet somehow connected. Perhaps through his mother who was in the Choir, President of the C.W.L. and very visible within the Church. So even though he wasn't there, it was kind of a nice ritual to do because my mother-in-law would say, "Oh, there are my grandchildren in Church." So there was a lot of pride wrapped up in that. I never took them to the United Church once I joined the Catholic Church. It was not a political decision. It was just the way it was and I was a Catechist and we just went Catholic all the way.

O.k., how would you describe your awakening to your lesbian identity?

Shocking! My 'Awakening', I can tell you it's just like when they say, "Do you remember where you were when J.F.K. was assassinated?" It's that kind of thing with me. It was in August 1992: I was looking out a window: I was a Camp Nurse for fifty-eight Girl Guides; I was in the Health Building; I looked out and I saw a woman and she was just kind of standing in the field, there were games going on, and that's when I realized that I had cells. Like… I just felt like…. That I had just come to life in parts of me that I had never felt before. I had a very physiological experience. So that was on a Saturday, and on a Sunday

I did something that I cannot, still, believe I did. I sat down with this woman, who was also a Guider at the time, and I told her how I felt about her. If somebody had told me the week before… the day before… that this was going to happen to me!!! I would have called them CRAZY. People used to call my husband and me, Barbie and Ken because we were so ecstatically perfect. So my 'Awakening' was very strong. I knew instantly what it was. It was as if I knew it all along, but had not addressed it. It's like… it was like a… meeting a bear… you think…what do I do?…do I play dead?…do I look this bear in the eye?…it was bigger than I was…there was nothing I could do, but to say 'hello' to the bear and go forward with that. It was very strong, very powerful, and it has never left me.

Were you able to share this identity with the people closest to you?

They knew instantly. They knew that something was up, as they have told me. It seems as though I just woke up. I've written it down once, that I think that my family saw that I had stars in my eyes. I just… they instantly knew what it was… because… at this time I was asking this person, I'll call Bea, to my home for tea and she would come and my parents, especially my mother, who's used to not sharing me, she instantly knew. I have two sisters and a brother, all younger than I am. I am ten years older than my youngest sibling. I am five and six years older than two sisters and ten years older than a brother. My brother didn't say very much for the first six years. My sisters would, kind of, attack me on the topic and I would deny it. I would be so evasive, which was a departure from the relationship we had which was extremely fun. So there was a lot of tension in the family that came as a result of the lying, on my part, and just in how they knew that I was completely different. Although… I still love my children and I love the idea of being a wife; having a home; running a home; working; volunteering. Something had changed that. There was a tension and there was resentment. There was… my family… I believe I alienated myself from my family. The time I spent with them, I was now spending with Bea. So that was 1992 when it started and they knew right away. They knew instantly what it was, which is very funny because we had never spoken about the words 'Lesbian, Gay, Homosexual' in our family. This is a family who does not even say "Oh, my God" because you just don't say "God" and you don't say "Oh, my God" instead you just say, "Oh, my goodness." So we had no language to talk about it. The way it played out was through alienation and through hard feelings. My sisters would either holler out at me face to face or call me up. I felt, and it came to light later, that there were great discussions about me in my family. My family is a matriarchal family. It is very strong. My grandmother, who is in her late eighties, heads the family. Every emotion, every feeling that ever arises in the family, she either procures it or deals with it for us. My mother is, pretty much, the same. So my father didn't ever say very much. My brother never said very much. Then it was a very really tense life, a very tense existence to do that. For some reason, what I wanted seemed to override the bond that I had with my family and I don't know why. It's not as if I didn't know what I was doing. By this time, Bea and I were having a love affair. So I came in as being lesbian to my husband and that was very difficult. He is very close with his mother. This was in 1995. I confirmed it with my family one year after I confirmed it with my husband. Interestingly, the connection to the Church there is very curious. The day that I told my husband, July 01, 1995, he went immediately to his mother and asked her what to do. She called me and said, "You will always be like a daughter." Whereas my family used the Church against me, my mother-in-law used the Church to welcome me.

Did you suffer any losses or were you celebrated in any way because of your lesbian identity?

I'll answer the easy one first. Celebrated as a lesbian – no, no never. That whole myth about Gay Pride! Well, Gay Pride is a myth to me, in my reality, in my experience. There is no pride at all, at this point, ten years later in 2002. I really have to fight hard against having shame. I guess the loss… even though in 1992, when I realized what happened to me, on that day in August. I've owned it ever since and I've not let it go. It's been a slow climb away from shame and I've lost a great deal…. I think I'll answer the next part… with my family… I have lost them! People say, "Oh, it's their loss." And I laugh to myself because I have a huge family; a huge family and a huge very gathering family; they meet a lot; they eat together; they nurture each other; and so on, and being excluded from that since 1996, that's six years ago, it's... very hurtful. Some days it bothers me more than other days, but it is something that is always with me, in everything that I do very much. I've lost... start with the future. Like, I've lost a future with a family that I was rooted in; I was born into. At present...here we are, it's New Year's Eve day and I have presents in my closet, that I have in case, in case they come and give me presents. They don't give me presents. They give my dog presents and my children presents. So those are the tangible losses. My sister, I think, just had a baby last month, I think. So this will be the only niece or nephew, I'm not sure which it is, that I haven't watched growing inside the belly; joking about; knitting or sewing things for. So it's that kind of loss at present. I have no idea about my family's health. I don't know how my grandmother is? I can't call her. I can't call her because there's still no language to speak to one another. Another thing, at present I'm in University and my Dad was in the Navy for thirty-eight years and so I would be eligible to have some kind of payment toward my schooling through the Armed Forces, but I can't even approach him for any help. So it's those kinds of tangible things. Some of the other things.... Alright... that was my present and future... perhaps my past... I don't have any baby pictures of myself. I think I was the most 'shot' child. Cameras were coming into vogue, in the early sixties, into the homes and I was born in 1958. The first grandchild and just doted on. I know there are hundreds of pictures and all of my books and I even know that clothing exists that I would love to have. Simply because it was a part of who I am. Two years ago, just to punctuate how missing I am from the family and how the family is missing from me, my sister, my baby sister, got married. An invitation came from her, to my once husband's address, and it said, "Any of you are invited." So I went with my daughter. So for the family photo shoot, my father told me, "So then, we'll see YOU back at the hall for the dinner?" I was not included in the family photo. This was a Church wedding. Interestingly enough, she married a man who was Catholic and she changed to Catholicism. So it's these kinds of things and I guess it's a blend of tangible and intangible.... It's a loss of not being able to go to the mall because I have been accosted by my family in the mall; on the phone, on the street.... I was stalked by my grandmother for about two years; at my home, at Bea's home; if we met, if I saw her as she drove by, my grandmother would stick her tongue out at me.... When I came in as being gay to my father and mother, my father got his hands on a Bible from somewhere because we didn't have a Bible growing up. We had cookbooks; but we didn't have a Bible. My father would quote the Bible for me. So the more he did that, the more I lost and, perhaps, the more he lost, as well. ... I was surprised to be able to go to the Church to attend the wedding, which I had spoken of earlier, because of how my father and mother and grandmother would tell me how evil I was. The very last thing that my grandmother said to me was, "I hope you die alone." I said, "Nan, dying alone I can handle...its living alone that's a real bitch." I would joke with my father and say, 'Dad, where did you get that Bible? You must have photocopied it?' We were a real teasing family, a joking family.... Still there was no room for me now because they say I'm evil and they have the proof to back it up from their Reverent. To back it up that I'm bad, I'm deviant, I'm perverted, and all of that. At that wedding, that I went to with my daughter, there were over one hundred fifty people just from my family alone. She, my sister, married a man from Newfoundland and he had just minimal family and so most of the guests were my family. I remember being so shy, and I had never been shy with my family. We were always joking and I remember looking at them... all of them. They were sat up at the tables together. There were my uncles, my cousins. I remember feeling like a collective loss. Prior to that, I think I only thought of them as individually.

I thought...oh, my God...so and so is on the phone, wouldn't I love to phone Dad... or...how do you make that white sauce... or... what did Nan put in your biscuits...you know? That wedding was kind of the collateral damage. It was like all the faces were there at once and it was very profound. Even though there was a cordial atmosphere towards me by my family, everything was very tense and I was very shy. My new brother-in-law, my baby sister's brand new husband, came in from out in the park, where my family had all had their family photo done, and he told me where I was to sit. It was at a table with his uncles and aunts. I had never met them before and I had never met him before that day, and never met his family. So there... my daughter and I... my daughter would have been nineteen almost twenty at that time, an adult... and I thought... if I had gone there alone... without her there... I would have gone. But the things we do for our children... we have to show an example of how to be good. That was very, very difficult. We stayed for a little bit of the dance. Of course, I had nobody to dance with. I wasn't forthcoming and nobody said "welcome back to the family"; nobody said anything. I was sort of like... a neighbor who was invited... had to be invited... but nobody knows them really well. I know I'm dwelling on the wedding part; but that really punctuated the collective loss regarding the family. So that was very, very hard. I often wonder where the pictures are of the family photo done in the park in Halifax. The beautiful park in that August... I often wonder what they look like... what those photos look like... what the language is now... if someone comes in and says, "oh, my goodness, look at the family"... does someone say, "Well, there is another daughter."... or whatever. Sometimes I, sort of, romanticize about how they might surround that. How my lie has become their lie, perhaps in a different context, but is there none the less.

How has the Church offered you pastoral care in the following?

- As you came to recognize your lesbian identity?

I would say it was absent and I would say it was self-induced. The Church I married into and I became a Catholic. Two of the priests there in the past fifteen years had been accused...excuse me, found guilty of molesting boys! So, I was very suspicious of Catholic priests. I did not seek their counsel at all and I felt that I just couldn't go there. I also felt, in light of my father having said he had spoken to Rev.... I felt as though that support wouldn't be there either. So I had no Church. I had no family and I had no Church… and I had nobody! I lost any neighbors; I lost anybody connected, I guess, with the Church…. I had been a Guider, a Girl Guider, for nine and a half years through the Alma Church and I had been told, "Don't come back." … So, everything, Church-related, for me was negative. …. So now, I'm not only suspicious of the Catholic Church and its views on homosexuality; but I'm also suspicious that perhaps the United Church, although great strides are being made in the United Church – I know that… I'm not there yet as far as really trusting. It will take some time… It really will…before I can go there again. I'm not sure I've even… I graduated from University in May, of this year 2002, and I was in a Church then. I find it very cynical now, when I'm in there. I look at the Stations of the Cross…We're just past Christmas, last week was Christmas week. I would drive and go and see houses with mangers and then they would have Santa Clauses just, sort of, leaned up against the mangers. I just find… I don't know if that part of me is just… gone… but for right now it's quite dormant!… Perhaps to get back to the question… the Church has not been helpful; but I think that is probably 100% because I have not sought any help from the Church. What the Church has shown me, I was so vulnerable anyway, is that I just couldn't open myself up to yet another barrage of, "Aren't you bad… Don't you care about your family… God this…God that… God forgives everyone?" So it will take some time. I can't even say that I don't believe in God, because I do believe in God. So, there's that struggle all the time. I was playing some Christmas carols for people and I played Santa Lucia. So there was all the Christmas stuff, but I felt very hypocritical playing Santa Lucia and also playing the Christmas carols and singing them. … I just felt doubtful. I almost want to be able to say that I don't believe in God… but I can't. Perhaps that's from my early childhood… where Church was very good. It was fun. I loved going to Sunday school and being from a rural area the Church was it. The Church was my social life and my parents, as well. Right now I think of it as a social construction… patriarchal…patronizing… stereotyping… controlling… oppressive. I'm sorry that I really can't… other than knowing that good things are done through the Church. That doesn't ring true for me, right now. To me the Church is something that people hide behind. Like my parents to justify their hatred of lesbians.... Imagine a minister... a minister of the United Church... allowing that to happen! Knowing that that has happened; but yet does not attempt to correct or whatever to undo that stereotype that lesbians are evil, deviant people!!! I have not changed as a person. I have not changed. So...

Ok, has the Church offered you pastoral care as you developed and maintained your lesbian relationship?

One, yeah, just one relationship. Again, it's because of me. It's because of me and my own decision not to go toward the Church. I was really hopeful four years ago, in 1998, when I started university at St. F.X. which is a Catholic based, Catholic founded university. I wanted to befriend the Church again. Within three months of the first month, that September 1998, I saw a poster and it had the date and time of this open seminar. The seminar was called the Catholics response to homosexuality. I was elated. I thought, 'Here...I've arrived at a place of enlightenment where people can actually have seminars.' I remember that I had to make an extra trip up just to go to this. A philosopher stood up and he said, "God tells us we should love everyone." (And I'm paraphrasing) "We should love prostitutes, drug dealers", and he listed a whole lot of people... who I... have trouble with not considering that they are deviant... not stereotyping. He said, "Therefore, we need to love the homosexuals, too." I remember that I don't even know what happened to me! I... he finished speaking and everyone was kind of... in shock... because of what he said. It was very negative. I... I stood up and said, 'This might not be my fifteen minutes of fame, but it might be the three that will get me there.' I asked him where do you spend 10%... do you give 10% of your earnings to the Church? Please do not answer that because how would you feel if we had a seminar about philosophers at St. F.X. who do not give that much to the Church? I said, 'There are people from

Africa here, so why don't we have the Catholic response to slavery?' To me it made as much or as little sense. It was just... it didn't make any sense. I asked him to ensure me, I said, 'I am just embarking on a degree that I have given up everything for just to be here. How can you ensure me, now that you know I am a lesbian, that I will be treated fairly in my marks and just as a person attending St. F.X.?' He was the only one in the room who kept his back to me the whole time. I said, 'I don't know where your God comes from, but my God would never turn his back on me and he would never send anyone to give me a message that would turn his back on me.' After that seminar, I sat down. After I finished speaking, I sat down and there were students there saying, "I'm gay and I want to know that my marks... I want to know that it won't be held against me." It seemed, as though, we now had a little bit of a... voice. There were about thirty people at this event. Interestingly enough, they only booked it at a place that could only sit about nine or ten around a small table in a little office, conference type room. Afterward there were some nuns, that were there, and they came up to me and said, "Oh, you are so brave" and all of this. There was a man, my age, a mature student, who was in my Philosophy Ethics class and he said, "That was the bravest thing I have ever seen anyone do." To me that was... I was thinking... brave?... Like no it wasn't... Right now, as I am sitting here, I would like to do it again. I would be more articulate. I would be more aware of what I was saying. The words were just coming. It's like when you put on a mask or a costume and the words they just come... they just come. Maybe that was like a... lesbian student mask... I don't know... but I became political and I remained political for four years at St. F.X. and very political. The Professors knew that I was gay. I wrote papers on being gay. I put a face on. That's what I said to this man, to his back, I said, 'I am here. I know I am here now. I am putting a face on homosexuality." That's what I did. I had no shame about it. I wasn't really proud of it. I was a little shy about it and it felt funny. I had never been out on that kind of a limb before. I did not find the Church there throughout that process. It was really on... about getting a divorce, losing a home, practically going bankrupt process of that part of my life. Again, I never felt that the Church was at St. F.X. even... what I was hoping to find.

How has the Church offered you pastoral care during painful times in your relationship – like times of death, illness, loss of a job, death of parents or dealing with the hatred of others?

Well, just following along, I just felt that I couldn't approach the Church. I had some traumatic times... like losing my family... losing my status as a wife... losing my home... being ill... but no priest or minister ever sought me out. I wasn't hard to find... I was very easy to find. Nobody from the Church, either Church, came... or called... or anything. It seemed as if I... died... or I was just gone. Often I would think... try to go through the grieving process, and I wouldn't pretend that all these people had gone, but I would feel like I had died. I don't know... but when you lose all these people, all at once, it's like a death. I couldn't ever imagine going to one of the priests because I was so suspicious of them. I couldn't imagine going to the United Church minister because I heard in the news all the controversy surrounding homosexuality. So through the process, I would say they were absent... of my own accord.

What has been your experience of the Church's teachings in reference to human sexuality?

Well... Oh, now that's interesting because, as you know, I was a Catechist for six years.

A Catechist is?

It was a Sunday school teacher in Catechism. So I taught each of my kid's grades, three years each, just so as I could be there with them. All of the teachings, the hand-outs, the little cut-outs, the activities, the scripts for the role play, were all heterosexual and based on a standard nuclear North American family – white man / woman, depicted either as a picture or in words. We were, as Catechists, given the Lesson that we had to teach. The father, the head; the mother, in the home and those children, all able, all working, all talking, seeing, all able. That, I guess, would be part of an answer to your question on teachings.

Yes... was there any overt teaching on homosexuality?

I would have to argue yes. I remember in both. My United Church upbringing... these words keep ringing in my ears... about 'Honor thy Mother and thy Father'... and that was carried into the teachings in Catholism. So, to me that is an obvious statement against Homosexuality. To me, it's very obvious. There was never anything that said that you must not go near people who are homosexual, or whatever. That was totally absent... totally not an alternative as a family... in both families.

Could you clarify what you mean by, "Honor thy Father and Mother?" How that seems, to you, to be a teaching against homosexuality?

Ok., in a couple of ways. I guess the most obvious, to me, was that I, somehow, dishonored my own mother and father by coming in as a lesbian. In another way, I dishonored my children. They are homophobic and they find it hard to honor me. My daughter has even questioned, you know, "I don't even feel that I should have been born, if you are a lesbian" So there is that trickle down effect. If the Church, both United and Catholic, are saying, "Honor thy Father and thy Mother" then I don't think any of us would confirm being gay or lesbian. It's very hard to go against your mother and your father. It's not what they expect for you... and maybe not what they want for themselves. You've rocked their boat... and maybe your own.

Ok, thanks... Anything more on that?

No.

Have you felt free to take your partner to Church or do you feel you must hide your relationship?

Oh definitely! You must hide the relationship. It has been a very rocky relationship because of the Church in many ways. Definitely hiding… hiding out. In one respect, I am not used to having a partner in Church because I was it. It was myself and my children. So I was a loner anyway with going to Church. I was the rural kid who was dropped off at the Church early so that I could go into choir practice before Church started. So I'm used to arriving and being at Church alone. So I don't really miss that anyway. It was funny though… a few years ago, Bea and I, we went to one of the Church's, locally, for a great big Christmas concert. I remember that I felt I couldn't get out of there fast enough. I was very uncomfortable being in the Church even though it was a lovely time and the performance was nice. I felt bad. I felt like everybody knew and I just felt funny… like I was doing something bad. We were just sitting there with these hundreds of people but I felt… I was just hoping that nobody that I knew was there… and that was only a concert! It was Christmas hymns that they were singing. They were singing Christmas carols. I just felt funny being in Church with her. I don't think we've been in Church since that, together, except for my graduation.

How do you experience your relationship with the Church at the present time?

Definitely alienated… definitely. Sometimes I get clichéd about it. I think I am creating my own Church with people I like… with people who like me. All of the spirit of the Church… and I think of the actual founding intent of the Church… to be giving and forgiving and loving. So it's kind of like… you built it. When you lose it then you rebuild with people very carefully. It's hard to let just anyone in… like before when I let everybody into my life. Now it's like a couple of arms length around me with feelers all the time. If somebody is what I call 'too Churchy'… one of my sister graduate students is very 'Churchy'. She expands about the evils of Sunday shopping and so on and so on and so on… She is not in this... sort of Church, let's say, that I am building for... kind of... myself... for my own comfort zone. Somehow, I just have come to... not...resent... not distrust really...but maybe it is distrust... but I am a bit leery of just even being around her. So I am very careful. There is no Church, as the Institution, in my life right now. However, I can't let go of the idea of Church. There's this notion of Church, especially at this time of year when everything is so Church-centered. It used to be such a happy time with the decorations, lots of family, lots of food, and so on. Being a divorced person, we now do the divorced Christmas. So the Christmas now, with my kids, is disjointed. I don't have anyone of my own family. So... it's... I...for some reason it's a very ambivalent relationship because I won't go near a Church, even at Christmas, but yet... for some reason... I just love the notion of Church. So, I guess, if I can extrapolate the spirit of the... good spots... in my memory about Church and somehow just live according to that. I guess then it must be some of... how I'm getting through this... and I still feel like I'm getting through it. I don't feel like... I have arrived... I am going to be political... anti-Church... and this and this and this. I just don't have that Church physically, right now.

And finally Jeanine, is there anything that you would like to say to the Church in reference to your lesbian identity?

Well...the United Church... I thought a lot about how my father and mother sat down with their minister. I thought a lot, over the last six years, about what he must have said to them and also what they must have said to him. I'm a believer in what is said can be taken out of context and used against people. I really... even though... that young minister counseled my family towards hating me... and I've been told that they hate me. They have told me that they hate me because of this and nothing else. I just think that there must be a better way of, and I hate to use the word policing but I'm going to, policing ministers in how they counsel families. I mean... my family... my family was very vulnerable, too... and they went, I'm sure, in good faith saying, "My God, what do we do...our daughter, who is our eldest daughter and she has children,... involved and so on... what should we do?"

My mother and I never had a good relationship, and so it was not surprising to me the way she reacted. My father, on the other hand, I just love my father. I love my mother too, but my father is very special. For him to use something out of context is very unlikely. It's very unlikely that my father would have cooked this up… to call me on; "Be fruitful and multiply" was one of them. There were about seventeen or nineteen passages and I remember four being repeated, but I can't remember what they were right now. So, given that my father is not one to speak out against anyone, but given that he did speak out against me. I really feel that that minister let down the United Church and the repercussions from that have been far-reaching in my family. If this minister had been more circumspect in how he counselled my family, I think things would be different today. I think he, perhaps, gave them the ammunition they wanted or something which I feel was very unfair. I feel it was also very unfair for others, other than me. First of all, for my family because they must be confused too… they go to Church… they're supposed to be forgiving… they listen to him preaching… but yet they're sitting there, looking up at him, and it's ok that he knows that they have disowned me. So to me, it's very anti-theological to what the United Church was telling me the first eighteen years of my life. So, I think if I was to say anything, in a nutshell, it would be to re-evaluate what is being edified by ministers as far as how to counsel and perhaps it might also be a personality thing. Maybe instead of prescribing things to say that it would be easier to begin by saying some proscriptive things: Don't lead the families of those gay people to believe that they can use the Bible as a weapon because it hurts… like nothing else. Right from… it makes everything and every one of us hypocritical… it makes my family hypocritical… it makes me feel hypocritical… It makes my going to the wedding, this big wedding that I spoke of, it must have made my sisters feel hypocritical. So it has created this whole area of doubt with us in how they were counselled. Those first weeks, and this was when they were counselled by him, I figure they were the most critical weeks of all. Anybody that raw, going to see a minister! He had better know how to handle those things… and… oh… I think that is one of the things that hurt most of all and that it can happen outside the family. I mean, I came from a family that my mother thought it was funny when my sister contracted herpes, and had been passing it on unbeknownst to her until she found out and did something about it. It was a joke, in the family, that my sister was doing this but it was ok. So, hypocritical activity follows into this because of the Church. Because of the Church, I am deviant; but never mind my sister who was infecting people. Due to the Church it is I who am deviant. The counselling should be better facilitated, better policed and maybe better standardized. This is not to say that any family fits the mold of another family. However, some kind of standard "Don't let them use the Bible as a weapon".

Well, thank you very much for this interview, Jeanine.

Elizabeth's Tape

What has been your connection with the Church?

Well, over the years… I don't have a connection with the Church now. At one point in my life when I felt it, I sort of left the Church. It had been quite a significant time in my life. It was probably before my late teens until I was late twenties that I was involved in the Church then, but I am no longer.

What kind of a Church was it?

It was a Baptist Church. I was related to a number of different types of Churches not just the Baptist Church. There was a Lutheran Church and then there was a little old English Anglican Church. There were many very different places and many very different Churches. It was not the same one each time. Yeah.

So did it nourish you? You felt?

I think at the time it was pretty interesting. I always felt it was a part of my development as an individual. That was part of something that I considered and looked at and wanted to know more about and find out what it was all about. I hadn't grown up in a family where we attended Church. It was very much a breaking away from the family setting and to do something that was very much about me seeking something. Perhaps it was something in myself that I was looking for and I looked at the Church to start with.

How would you describe your awakening to your lesbian identity?

It was very, very slow. I knew that I was definitely a lesbian growing up; but I didn't even know the word. I hadn't even… it wasn't even a word that I was familiar with. So it wasn't like I had come… no, it just wasn't something that meant anything. Did I know I was lesbian? No, I wouldn't have been noticing. I knew what my sexuality was as I was growing up but I did… I think I was in my mid to late twenties that I was very much conscious of that I was somehow different. I think it was not from the thrill of another woman, because I had feelings when I had my first love affair with a woman when I was at college in my early twenties. But I wouldn't have said we were lesbians at that time at all. I just loved her. It just seemed natural and she was another Christian woman and we both went to Church. She was very much tied into the Church and we really loved each other. I'm not sure how you… yeah, it was just… maybe we thought we were grabbing at something… I don't know. What was the question again?

How would you describe your awakening to your lesbian identity?

Yeah…So then I suppose I was in my thirties. I felt that, you know, I was more aware then and people were more open and talking more. There was a lot more dialogue. The word lesbian? We heard it, we read it, and it was very much a conscious kind of thing. Yes, this was what I was and there was no way I was going to be straight. Yeah.

Did it distress you to discover that?

No. But I knew you kept it a secret. I knew it wasn't something that you went out and told everybody about. It must have been something dirty. Something you didn't want spread around. It wasn't right. When I look back now, I know that – within the Church. The Church was always connected with lots of lesbians. It wasn't something that was ever talked about or discussed. It was just women loving other women, which is interesting… anyway…yeah.

Were you able to share this with the people closest to you – your family?

No, no, no, again it was just by me knowing that. I had to keep it. It was something that I didn't tell. It was something wrong with something. I wasn't the "norm". I wasn't going to be normal. Actually that was a very sad time, I think, for me. Just realizing that I had to be able to cover up. I think it was a very sad time for me to recognize that this was what would be the case at this time for me. Yeah.

Did you suffer any losses or were you celebrated in anyway because of your lesbian identity?

Because it was so secret, I don't think there was any room for celebration. There was nobody around me celebrating. There was nobody in my life that was. Getting to know the women that were lesbians, now that was good. That was nice to find that place of fellowship really. Another lesbian, I mean, now that was great.

What losses do you think you suffered?

I don't actually say losses, you know. I mean my first love; I'm going to call Helen. I lost her to a man. She went weird and that was a huge loss. That was a terrible loss. My heart was broken then. It was my very first love, a broken heart forever. Yeah. I'm not sure since that was a really significant loss and a terrible loss. As for other losses – I don't think there are any more losses.

What about your relationships with your family? Was it strained?

Yes, I mean yeah when you put it that way. It was never strained; but it was never comfortable. It must have been strained if it were never comfortable. I choose never to live near my folks because I wanted my own life. I felt they would never accept it. So I choose to work and live in different parts of the country where I could have my own life and they would never arrive unexpectedly or be in anyway around. So I kept it pretty much under wraps really. It's funny, you know, it kind of jogs your memory. It was a very, very sad time to not be able to be honest with my family and to keep everything hidden. It was a funny, old time.

How was the Church offering you pastoral care in identifying yourself as a lesbian?

No, no, never – never ever. I never ever went anywhere where there was a woman priest, for one thing. That might have been easier. Although I did get involved with a group of women and they were called "Women Aglow" and they were American, actually. I think the organization, as I recall, came out of the United States and they were really angelic and charismatic. Most of them knew that I was a lesbian. They all believed that I could be healed of it and I remember they used to pray for me. Pray that I would somehow be healed of my lesbianism. There was never anybody saying that it's o.k., it's fine just being who you are and there never will.

How has the Church offered you pastoral care as you developed and maintained your lesbian relationships?

No, neither really. There was never any interference. I remember when I was actually living with my friend Pat. We were living together and I was actually going to the local little Anglican Church. I would go off to Church and do my thing and return home to Pat and I remember the minister never came and visited not once. It was no big deal. It was like, you know, you're being ignored. It's insulting because you're not given credit for anything – for being anything. So that's what it felt like. I'm not saying this very well, am I?

Yes, I think you're doing fine.

Alright, o.k.. It's just that not having any kind of identity, you know, is worse than somebody pointing you out… it's like your ignored… you're in the shadow of things.

You are just kind of a non-person? Would you say that?

Yes, yes that's what I mean. Sort of nobody is saying, "O.k., you're a lesbian. What's this about, you know, what is this for you?" Nobody is asking any questions, just ignoring it really.

During painful times in your relationships, has the Church been any support or help?

Yeah… the people have. The people who have certain religious convictions or Christian convictions have been. People have been longer than the Church, per say, you know. The Institution of the Church, I would have to say "No, definitely not." People who attend the Church have been loving, caring, you know, so in villages.

What has been your experience of the Churches teachings in reference to human sexuality?

Well, if you talk to anybody about homosexuality then there's certainly texts that they will point to and say, "Here you go – its what it says – it's unacceptable." The teachings that I've only ever heard is that homosexuality is a sin. That it is not acceptable. I don't think I ever heard anybody preach about sexuality in a Church. I'm going back a ways trying to remember. No, I can't ever remember anyone preaching about sexuality except saying stuff around homosexuality, which is what the Church is teaching against. It's not good, unacceptable.

Have you felt free to take your partners to Church or must you hide the relationships?

No, we don't go. Pat and I have never been. Pat didn't go generally and probably never would again. I don't think that would be an issue, would it?

Would you have gone if you felt you could have gone as a couple?

Oh yeah, in fact we were in the Church. Bernadette and I did go to the Launch of the Gay and Lesbian, a directory or something, in the Church in Pictou that had been put on. We went for that evening. There were other people there. I never went to Church with my family or my lover or anyone.

How do you experience your relationship with the Church at the present time?

I don't really have a relationship with the Church. It's funny, you know, if you talk about the Church as an Institution then we, I don't. If we talk about you, as a friend... well, somebody that's within the Church... then we do have a relationship. So that's very important to me, too. So it's about people who have religious beliefs or Christian beliefs or convictions or whatever and they are part of the Church. They are here and I do have relationships with those people and the Church. So yeah, I do.

Through people? Through the people of the Church?

Yeah.

And finally, is there anything that you would like to say to the Church in reference to your Lesbian Identity?

(Laughter)... What I would like to say? I think it would be that you have an identity as an individual. My experience is that this has been ignored and my sexuality. There must be millions of people, like myself, that the Church has failed terribly. Maybe I would have been in a good place now if I had been cared about. If only the Church had cared. I think it never has, least I never felt it had. The hurt, I think, that you feel is such an important part in your life. It's your sexuality. It's grievous that it's just ignored. I don't know what would get me back into a Church right now. It's such a strong emphasis on the patriarchy in the Church too. There are women who sort of moved away from any kind of trust in the victory of it. That's a whole other issue really, around God and the Trinity and all the stuff that's tied up with Christianity, I think. Yeah, it would take a lot for me to turn to be in a Church. Yeah.

That's it? Thank you.

Yes, I think so.

CHAPTER SIX
Analysis of The Stories

Analysis of Betty's Interview

Betty is a person who grew up in the context of the Church; the Catholic Church. It very much shaped her family ethos. She states that she was "a good Catholic" until she was 13 years old. There seems to be a certain bitterness against the Church that emerged at this time, and she states that she had to be very intentional about extricating herself from her connection with the Church. She related that being part of the Church was part of the "house rules". So, Betty emerged from a highly religious background and yet by the time she enters puberty she has largely rejected it. She says she just couldn't believe what they were telling her and she wanted "out". There is no specific mention here of her sexuality being an issue, but she states that heterosexuality and exclusively heterosexual families were the only models celebrated and upheld in the Church of her youth. She sees no change in this area even today. When she attends weddings she finds the heterosexual rhetoric oppressive along with the lack of female imagery for God.

Betty says that she was quite involved in sports where she would not be relating to men much. This suited her fine. The early part of her life seems to have involved angry rebellion. Throughout the interview there is a lack of respect for the Church and a longing not to have a thing to do with it. She is very concerned that the definition of what constitutes a family be broadened by the Church to include those who are unable to conform to the traditional norm. An implicit message here might be that because of a certain lack of flexibility and shaming the Church has caused hardship for well-meaning, non-conventional people.

Betty's relationship with her family appears to be on a tolerance level rather than one of real sharing. She says "they know" she is a lesbian and they are very hospitable to any partner she may bring home, but they don't actually talk about lesbianism and how that might impact Betty's life. From an early age it would seem that, for Betty, her real family is formed from her friends. She has not desired to fit into the traditional family mold, at all and yet she cares greatly about her family-of-origin. Perhaps knowing the stance the Catholic Church has taken against homosexual persons, she feels that rather than push things she will simply live on the periphery; then things do not have to come to a head. This compromise seems to be workable for all concerned. The approval of her family-of-origin is not so important to Betty, at least that is what she purports.

Betty is a political activist and believes in the political process. She believes that the arena for social change is not the Church at all, but rather the secular, public realm. She, in some sense, sees the Church as anachronistic and really would not go to the Church for any help or guidance. She basically just wants the Church to stay out of her life and out of the body politic. There is no perception that the Church has anything to offer in the way of pastoral care. She has absolutely no intention of seeking help from the Church. Amen

Analysis of Pam's Interview

Pam has had an eclectic experience of the Church. She has sampled many denominations and has not chosen to join any. When she was a teenager, and part of a youth group, she thought she might join a Church, but then Church policy proved a hindrance. Pam had no one in her family who attended to the religious aspect of her upbringing. She went from pillar to post and never established any roots in the Church.

Pam came from a highly dysfunctional family where there was little respect and much psychological as well as physical abuse. Her mother was the family scapegoat and her father used anything to bring charges of inadequacy against her. Pam firmly believed that she could not make her sexual identity known in the family or her mother would be blamed and abused because of it. Within this family system the presence of a loving, caring God was not evident to the members of the family. There is a sense in which the family is left to deal alone with great unleashed evil with no support from anywhere, and certainly no help from the Church. The family lived with a shameful secret already and Pam did not want any more shame brought into the family because of her sexuality. In her family culture there was a definite causal connection between homosexuality and filthy, disgusting behaviour. Pam believes there is some measure of responsibility for this shaming to be laid at the doorstep of Christianity. She has witnessed anti-homosexual rhetoric on the television from TV evangelists who mostly come on the screen in the early morning hours. They say just what they like and no one stops them. Once again God is not in any way a restraining presence. This further entrenches Pam's belief that God is largely ineffectual and largely irrelevant. She does not in any way look to the Church for support, succor, or nurturance. Having worked for most of her adult life with troubled youth, Pam has been exposed to some extremely dysfunctional situations. She refers to them as evil and she has not seen the presence of God amidst the abuse and heartache. She does not even expect God to be there. In her world everyone is "at sea" in a storm with no support or help from God or the Church.

Pam is very insistent that the Church stop interfering in the identify formation process in young people vis-à-vis their sexuality. She feels that young adulthood is a time of legitimate searching. She is very upset about the shaming that some denominations have heaped upon homosexual young people. She feels the Church must accept some responsibility for driving them to suicide and turning their friends and family against them. The Church is not perceived by Pam as a loving agent of a loving God, but rather an agent of evil representing a largely indifferent God. Pam believes that religion has done and continues to perpetrate great evil in the world. She sees the Church as a place of little compassion or understanding of those who, in all sincerity, cannot fit the heterosexual model that has been the template for the Christian understanding of human sexuality for centuries. This has been based on particular understanding of the Bible dealing with the order of creation.

Pam has been greatly affected by her dysfunctional family situation. It colours her perspective on the whole of life. She was forced to live with tremendous assault on all that is decent and sacred in life. Her mother was desecrated. Her home was a war zone. She has unspeakable anger against her father. The Church, in large measure, envisions God as a male father figure. It could be argued that she is unable to relate to this image of God and yet is mad at God for not being the loving father she should have had as a child. When this God is seemingly absent and this God condemns her very being, she feels she has no choice but to totally and completely reject God and the Church. She just wants to be left alone.

Perhaps pastoral care in this instance might involve the modeling of a less punitive male deity. This model, out of the Old Testament, is still very operative today in some churches and is touted in loud, abusive tones from some pulpits. Also, pastoral care might involve the Church acquainting itself with current understandings of human sexuality without using the pulpit as a forum of shame for those who feel called along a different path. Support on the part of the Church for those who must deal with societal condemnation and degradation on an ongoing basis might help someone like Pam in the future.

Pam, however, will not be seeking pastoral care any time soon from a Church. She considers the Church largely ineffectual and responsible for creating a climate of condemnation for homosexual persons.

Analysis of Joy's Interview

Joy's experience of the Church has been largely positive and stabilizing. She loves her Church community and she loves the Church building. For her it is definitely her spiritual home and she is very committed to it. As we look back over her life in the Church, she is very grateful for the wonderful groups she belonged to and the nurturance she received from various members of the Church and various ministers over the years.

Joy's family system is very much intertwined with the Church. Had this particular Church condemned her sexuality it would have been excruciating for her. Instead, she had been met with love and support. The incident with the friends of the family who were long-time members of the Church pained Joy greatly, but she was able to objectify the incident enough to feel that she could remain a part of that Church. The individual minister in this case was supportive to the point of self-sacrifice, which spoke of love and caring to Joy and her partner.

Joy is saddened by the lack of wholehearted celebration of lesbians in the Church and the lack of safety for some lesbian leaders in the Church. She feels that the Church has progressed a great deal on this issue, but has a long way to go. She also feels much of the root cause of homophobia is fear and hopes some day to help allay that fear through the formation of informational groups or something similar.

Joy has a long-standing love relationship with her Church. The listener can feel and sense the joy and the strength that the Church has given her. Although her family-of-origin has not always supported her lesbian relationships, she feels that the Church family has, in a very real way, given her the strength to carry on in the face of familial and societal adversity. She has absolutely no intention of leaving the Church and plans to deepen her commitment when she has more free time. For Joy, to be known and loved for who she is is an important value. In her Church she feels she does not have to hide her identity in any shameful way, and she celebrates that reality. She doesn't flaunt her sexuality, she just is who she is and that is enough.

In my opinion, Joy has received excellent pastoral care from the Church from her very earliest days. She did not experience rejection because she did not follow the heterosexual model. She was not faced with the grief of losing her faith community, but instead has found the Church to be a place of great joy and happiness for her. She is fully integrated into the life of the Church community and fulfils her part as a functioning member of the Body of Christ. Sexual conformity has not been forced upon her and she has not been forced to choose between the Church and her life.

Analysis of Mary's Interview

Mary has been nurtured by the Catholic Church for most of her life. Recently she decided to affiliate herself with the United Church because they accept her as a lesbian. For her the decision to leave the Catholic Church was very logical. Because anything other than heterosexuality was not accepted she made the logical choice to change denominations. For Mary, her involvement in the Church has been very task-oriented, ie decorating the Church for Christmas, etc. There is the mention of a previous lack of peace, which she finds now when she sits quietly and lights a candle in both traditions. Mary has strong connections with the Catholic Church through her family. Because of their strong ties to the Catholic Church, which has a policy of the condemnation of homosexual persons, she fully expected that she would be rejected by them. This seemed totally logical to her. She was, however, surprised to learn that her family accepted her as a lesbian in spite of Church teachings. This has been a great joy to her, but she was prepared to be rejected. There was no plan to give up her lesbianism in order to conform to Church teachings or to be accepted by her family. There is a core strength there that, ironically, has probably come from her faith.

Mary seems to think of the Church in legalistic terms. The Church has certain rules that you are expected to follow and if you can't follow those rules you find a Church with different rules. It is all very logical; very straightforward. No mention is made of the emotional pain of rejection by the Church of one's childhood and its profound relationship to the soul of a person. Mary is not in touch with the emotional grief of having to leave the Catholic Church.

There is also a naïve belief that secular laws that apply to the human rights of people of different genders and orientations have to be adopted by the Church. The Church operates on the "ultra vires" principle. The Church is above the law and can deny anything it wants to anybody given enough scriptural or theoretical rationale.

For Mary, marriage is an important thing. It is something she is very committed to and believes in. It has been painful for her to be denied marriage by the Church because she would want to marry a woman. She has great hope, however, that once the secular society passes gay marriage into law, the Church will follow suit. Once again, her mind is operating along the lines of legalism.

Mary loves the Church. She wants to be involved in it on a very deeply active level. She is there to help with Church suppers, worship, and confirmation classes. Whatever. When she speaks of the Church it is with great joy and enthusiasm. Mary loves to be part of the Church community, helping out wherever she can. She and her partner are well accepted and loved where they attend Church. They have not asked to be married there though as they feel this would upset some people. The Church has no clear policy on homosexual marriage.

The Church has made a big difference in Mary's life. She finds a place of belonging and sustenance there. Various clergy over the years from both the Catholic and the United Church have supported her as she lives her lesbian identity. She has had countless opportunities to offer her gifts to the Church and no one has kept her from doing that. Mary sees the Church as a big part of her future. Her commitment is only going to grow stronger. She is a woman of strong faith.

Analysis of Jeanine's Interview

Jeanine is a person for whom the institutional Church has played a major role. Right from childhood on into her middle years, she belonged to various groups within the Church. It has all meant a great deal to her, giving her life purpose and joy. What she discovered, however, was that within her particular traditions unless you "coloured inside the lines" or lived a life of traditional conventional understanding, the respectable religious life could unravel in a very dramatic way. Certain realities bore the stench of shame in the Church. One was divorce, the other homosexuality.

It is interesting to note that Jeanine was able to function very well in a heterosexual context. There is no mention of long years of angst and soul-searching. No, Jeanine was very involved in her Church, her family, Girl Guides, her marriage, etc. She even notes that the marriage was very harmonious and that she and her husband were well-suited and had a happy family life very connected to both families of origin. Both families were matriarchal with the mothers and grandmothers very involved in the Church. Jeanine was part of this matriarchal family system and as the eldest daughter would have been in quite a position of power and trust. As a nurse she also would bear a great deal of responsibility. Her influence would have been extensive in the community, at work, and at home. The fact that her husband demonstrated no spiritual leadership and deferred to the women in this matter seemed quite normal to Jeanine, as her father followed the same pattern. One has the image of a family where the women are clearly defined and in the forefront and the men as hazy, shadowy figures in the background. The nurturance and the care of the children was clearly in the hands of the women. Jeanine loved the role of wife and mother. She loved being part of organizing church suppers. She loved teaching faith-development classes and ushering young people into the Church. Her life was good. She had a sense of purpose and belonging and there was little or no malaise on her part. She played her rôle very well.

Then one day it all changed. A seismic shift. She looked out a window; saw a person she was tremendously attracted to, and her whole life changed. She fell in love. The object of her affection was not a man as would be expected given her history. It was a woman her age leading some young people in a game. She describes the experience as an awakening; as if she had been asleep previously. All her bodily systems responded and she felt compelled to go with what was happening. She had, however, in the recesses of her being known she was a lesbian. She writes, "I knew instantly what it was. It was as if I knew it all along, but had not addressed it." Sometimes the heterosexual conditioning can be very strong and the lesbian identity suppressed for many years until there is a sudden or gradual breakthrough. In this case it was sudden.

Of course, Jeanine's life and the life of those close to her was thrown into a free fall. Everything came unglued! The marriage. The relationship with her family. Her life in the community. Everything. She was greatly loved and there must've been a strong measure of shock, disbelief, and grief. The first reaction would be to try to return things to normal. That wasn't going to happen. Jeanine persisted. Her family-of-origin, who were nominal Christians at the best of times, all of a sudden become very religious. They co-opted an inexperienced and uninformed minister to help them in their plight. Jeanine needed to be brought back to her senses and reined-in.

The Bible would be the best tool. The minister armed them with quotes from the Bible, taken entirely out of their cultural context, condemning homosexuality. The family seized on this as a control mechanism. The father, who had shown very little familial leadership in the past, was suddenly an expert on the Bible quoting the passages the minister had armed him with. The family knew Jeanine was a highly religious person, so they went to the Church to deal with this situation. Jeanine was labeled evil. She was shunned. She was unrepentant and therefore put outside the family circle. No one was to have anything to do with her. She was a disgrace. Jeanine was shocked at their reaction. She had always felt so loved and celebrated in her family. Now she was a thing to be scorned. She grieved for the happy times, but there is no turning back. The Christmas presents are still in the closet in case they surprised her with a visit. But they never do.

In this instance, it would seem to me that the Church was being used as a way to control and shame Jeanine. The family is not really caring about Jeanine's soul as much as they are caring about keeping the status quo. She was so good; so dutiful, now this. The Church must be wary of being used to promote someone's agenda. The Church can be an unsuspecting pawn in many a familial game. The father has, heretofore, been a rather weak figure in the family configuration. There has been a very close bond between Jeanine and her father, but not her mother. Perhaps her mother had always been very jealous of this alliance, seeing it as a threat to her marriage. Her husband has perhaps been more closely aligned with Jeanine than to her. This situation may have gone on for years and the mother secretly resented it. Perhaps she is tired of having to always take the leadership role in the family. Along comes this situation. Clearly a betrayal of all that is decent and right. It is time for her husband to play the man and condemn what is evil, keeping it from sullying the rest of the family. The evil thing is thrown out. The father has finally played the manly part. Husband and wife are united in dealing with this threat to their family name. The Church was used for backup and authority.

Jeanine has always been the "good" girl. She has always tried to bring honour to her family through her various activities and it is very painful for her to bring shame just because she loves a woman. This perhaps explains her fury at the person at the college who classed homosexual people with all manner of low life. She reacted to this because she knows she has tried to live an upright life according to the teachings of the Church, and to be an example of a noble Christian woman. To have her dignity and honour shorn from her because of her sexuality is grievous to her. She protests greatly in this instance and on other occasions during her years at the Catholic College. She has tried to honour her father and mother and to be a mother her children can honour. She feels the Church has stolen honour from her and it hurts.

Jeanine has cut all ties with the Church. Whether she will ever return is unknown at this point. She is angry with the way the Church used its position and authority to condemn her, to label her, and condemn her to live a life of guilt, grief, and shame. The loss of the Church in her life has been a profound loss for Jeanine. She was steeped in the Church and dedicated her life to it. She also brought her children up in the Church. Now she grieves because they are being taught to condemn their mother.

Jeanine is angry. She is hurting. She is disgusted. She still believes in God, but wants nothing to do with the institutional Church. She has no trust in the clergy and she believes all of the teachings are based on one familial model and one model only – the patriarchal heterosexual, white, able-bodied model. No room for any deviation whatsoever.

Pastoral care, in this instance, would involve the counselee venting feelings through storytelling, and allowing the person to state their truth as they see it without condemnation; and a show of caring while respecting their need and desire not to be part of the Church at this present time.

Analysis of Elizabeth's Interview

Elizabeth is a person who was not brought up in the Church. When she began the process of identity-formation in her late teens and early twenties, she decided to explore what the Church had to offer. She found an outlet for her gifts and she found love and acceptance by various Church people. At one point she was quite deeply involved in a charismatic branch of the Church and was a member of "Women Aglow", which is a charismatic Christian organization.

Elizabeth does not display any animosity towards the Church apart from feeling largely ignored and consigned to the shadows. This may have been largely due to her perceived status as a single woman more than anything else. As her self-realization in the area of her sexuality developed she shared this information with the "Woman Aglow". They did not reject her in any overtly hostile manner, but she was informed that her sexuality was not acceptable, and they prayed for healing for her. They were not viciously self-righteous or judgmental, only non-accepting. Elizabeth found great fellowship and Christian community in this group, but as her life has progressed has not chosen to re-affiliate.

Upon the gradual emergence of Elizabeth's understanding of her sexuality she felt instinctively that it was not something her family would or could accept. This lack of acceptance was not in an overt way emanating from the Church because this family was not a Church-going family. But it was part of the culture, which was built upon the foundations of Christianity. She believed there would be shame, disgust, and rejection from her family so she was intentional about managing their relationship in such a way that her "secret" would never be revealed. She felt very sad about having to keep her family at bay because she loved them very much. All through the years she never cut ties with them, but shared only part of her life with them. The arrangement was emotionally draining and painful for her, but she believed at the time that it was the only workable solution.

There does not seem to be a strong desire on the part of Elizabeth to live out her spirituality through the Church at this time in her life. She is not resentful against it, but wishes the Church had been more proactive in honouring her identity and choice of partner. She saw other couples being visited and validated, but not her and her partner. They were nobodies. She does not expect or want anything from the Church at this time. She does, however, respect the choice of other people to affiliate themselves, and is grateful for the love and caring that individual Christians have offered on countless occasions. There is a lingering regret that when she was younger she was left to flounder on her own as she dealt with her sexuality. She feels the Church could have shown more caring as opposed to benign neglect. Of course, there is the gratitude that she wasn't overtly persecuted and labeled a witch or something worse.

There is a wistful sadness when Elizabeth speaks of the Church; a sense of regret in reference to "what could have been".

Conclusion

I began my research with the thesis that the Christian Church has made life difficult for lesbian women and that the pastoral care they have received from the Church has been inadequate and punitive. I interviewed six lesbian women in reference to their experience with the Church. Rather than a uniform response, I received a varied response. There has been uniformed teaching about lesbians by the Church. There has been neglect and a lack of respectful insight into their reality. There has been shunning. There has been ignorance. However, there has also been some excellent pastoral care. Some of the clergy have proven to be highly educated in the area of human sexuality and have stood in solidarity with some of the women. Others have stood by their side during those transitional and painful times that are a part of every life. Some congregations have offered a wonderful welcome and inclusion. Some parishioners have gone out of their way to be kind and supportive. Many more are making the effort to understand and help lesbian persons.

For some members of this research the Church has no meaning. They want no part of it, and just wish parts of it would cease from anti-homosexual rhetoric. Instead of being rejected by the Church they have rejected the Church. For others in this study the Church has a central meaning in their lives and they long for full, celebrated, dignified inclusion.

For me personally, I began this research with a deep sense of despair and hopelessness. I assumed that the picture was all black. After having gone through this process I am delighted to state that the picture is hardly as dark and bleak as I had thought. Lesbian women are taking their place in the Church, and are receiving some excellent pastoral care even from pastors, who in all sincerity are not able to approve of their way of being. There is an increasing recognition that we all must follow our own personal conscience. There is also an increasing respect for a person's right to decide for themselves whom they will love without condemnation for that choice.

I have found this work excruciating, painful, and heartbreaking. I have also found, to my wondrous surprise, signs of hope, love, and great and precious caring.

Endnotes

1. Paul A. Tournier, <u>Listening Ear, Reflections on Christian Caring</u>, (Minneapolis, MN: Augsburg Publishing House: 1987), p.19.

2. Anton T. Boisen, <u>Christian Perfectionism</u>, Chicago Theological Register (January 1934): 12. All biblical texts are from the New Jerusalem Bible: Reader's Edition (New York: Doubleday, 1990) unless otherwise noted.

3. Walter M. Abbott, ed., <u>Pastoral Constitution on the Church in the Modern World</u>, The Documents of Vatican II, S.J. (New York: America Press, 1966), p. 213.

4. John J. McNeill, Freedom, Glorious Freedom, (Boston: Beacon Press, 1995), p. 28.

5. Thomas S.J. Gertler, <u>East Germany: A Spiritual Discernment</u>, (America, 1991), p. 88.

6. John McNeill, <u>The Blondelian Synthesis</u>, (Leiden, Hollard: E.J. Brill, 1966), p. 182-183.

7. Clinton R. Jones, <u>Understanding Gay Relatives and Friends</u>, (N.Y.: The Seabury Press, 1978), p. 40.

8. Ibid., p. 40.

9. Ibid., p. 40.

10 Wayne E. Oates, Grief, Transition, and Loss, (Minneapolis: Fortress Press, 1997), p. 31.

11 John J. McNeill, Taking A Chance in God: Liberating Theology for Gays, lesbians, and Their Lovers and Friends, (Boston: Beacon Press, 1988), p. 54.

12 Ibid., p. 174.

13 Larry Kent Graham, Discovering Images of God: Narratives of Care, Among Lesbians and Gays, (Kentucky: Westminster John Knox Press, 1997), p. 39.

14 John Fortunato, Embracing the Exile: Healing Journeys of Gay Christians, (San Francisco: Harper and Row, 1984), p. x.

15 James B. Nelson, Between Two Gardens: Reflections on Sexuality and Religious Experience, (New York: The Pilgrim Press, 1983), p. 118-119.

16 McNeill, p. 31.

17 McNeill, p. 32.

18 McNeill, p. 33.

19 McNeill, p. 35.

20 McNeill, p. 37.

21 McNeill, p. 38.

22 David and Shirley Switzer, Parents of the Homosexual, (Philadelphia: The Westminster Press, 1980), p. 70.

23 Ibid., p. 71.

24 C. Murray Parkes, First Year of Bereavement, (Psychiatry 33, 1970), p. 448., and David K. Switzer, Coming Out as Parents: You and Your Homosexual Child, (Louisville: Westminster John Knox, 1996), Chapters 1 and 2.

25 David K. Switzer, Pastoral Care of Gays, Lesbians, and Their Families, (Minneapolis: Fortress Press), p. 119.

26 Ibid., p. 119.

27 Ibid., p. 119.

28 Ibid., p. 119.

29 Ibid., p. 120.

30 Ibid., p. 120-121.

31 Ibid., p. 121.

32 Ibid., Switzer, 121.

33 John J. McNeill, Taking A Chance On God, (Boston: Beacon Press, 1988), p. 96.

34 Ibid., p. 96. (Ez. 16:48-50).

35 McNeill, p. 97.

36 McNeill, p. 97.

37 Henri Nouwen, The Wounded Healer: Ministry in Contemporary Society, (Garden City, N.Y.: Image Books, 1979), p. 89.

38 McNeill, p. 97.

39 McNeill, p. 98.

40 John J. McNeill, The Church and the Homosexual, revised and expanded edition (Boston: Beacon Press, 1988), McNeill, Taking A Chance on God, (Boston: Beacon Press, 1988), p. 92.

41 John J. McNeill, Freedom, Glorious Freedom: The Spiritual Journey to the Fullness of Life for Gays, Lesbian, and Everybody Else, (Boston: Beacon Press, 1995), p. 147.

42 J. Fortuanto, Embracing the Exile: Healing Journeys of Gay Christians, (San Francisco: Harper and Row, 1982), p. 247.

43 Richard D. Parsons and Roberts J. Wicks, editors, Clinical Handbook of Pastoral Counseling Volume 2 (N.Y.: Paulist Press, 1993), p. 229.

44 Ibid., p. 230.

⁴⁵ Carter Heyward, <u>Heterosexist Theology: Being Above It All</u>, Journal of Feminist Studies in Religion 3 (1987), p. 29-38, Ibid., p. 237.

⁴⁶ William R. White, <u>Stories for the Telling</u>, (Minneapolis: Augsburg Publishing House, 1986), p. 70-71.

⁴⁷ Richard D. Parsons and Robert J. Wicks, editors, <u>Clinical Handbook of Pastoral Counseling</u>, Volume 2 (N.Y.: Paulist Press, 2003), p. 234.

Appendix A
THESIS PROPOSAL AND QUESTIONS FOR INTERVIEWS

To Whom It May Concern

I will be conducting a project involving qualitative research in the form of an interview process. The questions will be the following:

1. What has been your connection with the Church?
2. How would you describe your awakening to your lesbian identity?
3. Were you able to share this identity with the people closest to you?
4. Did you suffer any losses or were you celebrated in any way because of your lesbian identity?
5. How was the Church helpful or hurtful in the following:
6. As you came to recognize your lesbian identity?
7. As you developed and maintained your lesbian relationships?
8. During painful times in your relationships? ie: death, illness, loss of job, death of parents, dealing with the hatred of others?

9. What has been your experience of the Church's teachings in reference to human sexuality?
10. Have you felt free to take your partner to Church or do you feel you must hide your relationship?
11. How do you experience your relationship with the Church at the present time?
12. Is there anything you would like to say to the Church in reference to your lesbian identity?

Bibliography

Adams, James Luther, Seward Hiltner, ed. *Pastoral Care in the Liberal Churches*. Nashville: Abingdon Press, 1970.

Adelman, Marcy, ed. *Midlife Lesbian Relationships: Friends, Lovers, Children, and Parents*. New York: Harrington Park Press, 2000.

Aden, Leroy, Harold J. Ellens (editors). *The Church and Pastoral Care*. Grand Rapids, Michigan: Baker Book House, c1988.

Alexander, Marilyn Bennett and James Preston. *We Were Baptized Too: Claiming God's Grace for Lesbians and Gays*. Louisville: Westminster John Knox Press, 1996.

Alpert, Rebecca T. "In God's Image: Coming to terms with Leviticus (Lev. 18:22; 20; 13)". *Twice Blessed*. Boston: Beacon Press (1989): 61-70.

Aetman, Dennis. *Homosexual Oppression and Liberation*. New York: Avon Books, 1971.

Appiah, K. Anthony. "The Marry Kind." *The New York Review of Books*, 20 June 1996, 48-54.

Armstrong, Peter, John Pearce. *The Anglican Church and Same Sex Couples*. Halifax, N.S.: Printers, Dal Printing, 1995.

Atkinson, Roberts. *The Life Story Interview.* Thousand Oaks, California: Sage Publications, 1998.

Augsburger, David W. *Anger and Assertiveness In Pastoral Care.* Philadelphia: Fortress Press, 1979. BV 4012.2 A93.

Bailey, D.S.. *Homosexuality and the Western Tradition.* London: Longmans, Grun, 1955.

Baker Millar, Jean. *What Do We Mean By Relationships?* Work in Progress. No 22. Wellesley: The Stone Center Working Paper Series, 1986.

Balka, Christie and Amy Rose ed. *Twice Blessed: On Being Lesbian or Gay and Jewish.* Boston: Beacon Press, 1989.

Bane, J. Donald. *Death and Ministry: Pastoral Care of the Dying and the Bereaved.* New York: Seabury Press, 1975.

Barrington, Judith ed. "The Erotic as Sacred Power: A Lesbian Feminist Theological Perspective". *In An Intimate Wilderness: Lesbian Writers on Sexuality*, ed. Judith Barrington. Oregon: The Eighth Mountain Press, 1991.

Beavers, Robert W. *Psychotherapy and Growth: A Family Systems Perspective.* New York: Brunner/Mazel, 1977.

Bell, Alan P. and MS Weinbery. *Homosexualities: A Study of Diversity Among Men and Women.* New York: Simon & Schuster, 1978.

Bergler, Edmund. *Homosexuality: Disease or Way of Life?* New York: Macmillan, 1962.

Berzon, Betty. *Permanent Partners: Building Gay and Lesbian Relationships That Last.* New York: E.P. Dutton, 1988.

Bevans, Stephen B. *Models of Contextual Theology.* New York: Orbis Books, 1992.

Blaney, Robert W. *Homophobia/Heterosexism and Lesbian/Gay Experience: An Annotated Bibliography.* Annual of the Society of Christian Ethics, 1987, The Knoxville, Tenn: Society of Christian Ethics, 1987, p. 229-252. Essay Libraries 277.

Boff, Leonardo. *Liberating Grace.* New York: Orbis Books, 1981.

Bons-Storm, Riet. *The Incredible Woman: Listening to Women's Silences in Pastoral Care and Counseling.* Foreward by Pamela D. Couture. Nashville, Tenn.: Abingdon Press, c1996.

Boogaart, Thomas A., Caroline J. Simon. *Walking & Talking with Homosexual Brothers and Sisters*: (Reformed context). Perspectives 12, p. 4-5, 8-16, Article, Libraries 227, 1998.

Borg, Marcus. "Homosexuality in the New Testament." *Bi cxble Review.* 10 (D1994): 20-54.

Borg, Marcus. *The God We Never Knew: Beyond Dogmatic Religion to a More Authentic Contemporary Daith.* San Francisco, CA. Harper SanFrancisco, 1997.

Boswell, John. *Christianity, Social Tolerance, and Homosexuality.* Chicago: The University of Chicago Press, 1980.

Boswell, John. *Christianity, Social Tolerance, and Homosexuality: Gay People in Western Europe from the Beginning of the Christian Era to the Fourteenth Century.* Chicago: University of Chicago Press, 1980.

Boyle, Sally. *Embracing the Exile: A Lesbian Model of Pastoral Care.* Toronto: The United Church Publishing House, 1995.

Bradshaw, John. *Healing the Shame That Binds You.* Florida: Health Communications Inc., 1988.

Brash, Alan A. *Facing Our Differences: The Churches and Their Gay and Lesbian Members.* Risk no 68, p. vii-xii, 1-75: Article, 1995.

Brooks, Virginia R. *Minority Stress and Lesbian Women.* Lexington, Massachusetts: Lexington Books, c1981.

Browning, Don S. *The Moral Context of Pastoral Care.* Philadelphia: Westminster Press, c1976.

Browning, Don S. *Toward a Practical Theology of Care*: (Vosburgh Lectures, 1982).Drew Gateway 53 No. 2. Libraries: 108, 1983, p 1-22.

Browning, Don S. "Rethinking Homosexuality." *Review of the Construction of Homosexuality*, by David Greenberg. *The Christian Century*, 11 October 1989, 911-16.

Buber, Martin, *I and Thou.* London: Fontana Press, 1958.

Buxton, Amity P. *Other Side of the Closet: The Coming-Out Crisis for Straight Spouses and Families.* Rev. ed. New York: John Wiley & Sons, 1994.

Capps, Donald. *Pastoral Care: A Thematic Approach.* Philadelphia: Westminster Press, c1979.

Carroll, William. "God as Unloving Father." *The Christian Century*, 5 March 1991, 255.

Catholic Church. Archdiocese of San Francisco, California. Senate of Priests. *Ministry and Homosexuality in the Archdiocese of San Francisco.* San Francisco: Senate of Priests, Archdiocese of San Francisco, 1983.

Chandler, Barbara, *Sexual Healing?*: (ministries to ex-gays and lesbians; bibliog.) Daughters of Sarah 22, p. 36-38, Article: Libraries 181, 1996.

Clark, J. Michael, Joanne C. Brown, and Lorna M. Hochstein. "Institutional Religion and Gay/Lesbian Oppression." *Marriage and Family Review* 14, issue 3-4 (1989): 265-84.

Clark, Neville. *Pastoral Care in Context: An Essay in Pastoral Theology.* Bury St. Edmunds: Kevin Mayhew, 1992.

Cleaver, Richard. *Know My Name: A Gay Liberation Theology.* Kentucky: Westminster John Knox Press, 1995.

Clinebell, Charlotte Holt. *Counselling For Liberation.* Philadelphia: Fortress Press, 1976.

Clinebell, Howard John. *Mental Health Through Christian Community; The Local Church's Ministry of Growth and Healing.* New York: Abingdon Press, 1965.

Clinebell, Howard John. *The Intimate Marriage.* New York: Harper & Row, 1970.

Clinebell, Howard John. *Growth Counseling for Mid-years Couples.* Philadelphia: Fortress Press, 1977.

Clinebell, Howard. *Basic Types of Pastoral Care and Counselling.* Nashville: Abingdon Press, 1984.

Clinebell, Howard. *Basic Types of Pastoral Care and Counselling.* (Revised and Enlarged Edition). Nashville: Abingdon Press, 1984.

Clunis, Merilee D., G. Dorsey Green. *Lesbian Couples.* Seattle, WA: Seal Press, 1988.

Coleman, Gerald D. *Pastoral Care of Homosexual Persons.* New York: Garland, 1992.

Coleman, Gerald D. *Homosexuality: Catholic Teaching and Pastoral Practice.* New York: Paulist Press, 1995.

Coleman, Peter. *Gay Christians: A Moral Dilemma.* Philadelphia, PA: Trinity Press International, 1989.

Comstock, Gary David. *Gay Theology Without Apology.* Cleveland. Ohio: Pilgrim Press, 1993.

Congregation of the Doctrine of the Faith. *Letter to the Bishops of the Catholic Church on the Pastoral Care of Homosexual Persons.* Given at Rome, 1 October, 1986.

Conn, Joann Wolski, ed. *Women's Spirituality: Resources for Christian Development.* New York: Paulist Press, c1986.

Couture, Pamela D. and Rodney J. Hunter, editors. *Pastoral Care and Social Conflict.* Nashville: Abingdon Press, 1995.

Crawley, David. *A Parish Transformed: (by changing community, gay-positive ministry). Our Selves, Our Souls and Bodies.* Boston: Crowley Pubications, p. 201-205, 1996.

Crites, Stephen. *The Narrative Quality of Experience.* Journal of the American Academy of Religion, pp. 290-307, 1971.

Crossan, John Dominic. *The Dark Internal: Towards a Theology of Story.* Allen, Texas: Argus Communications, 1975.

Cruikshank, Margaret, (editor). *Lesbian Studies: Present and Future.* Old Westbury, New York: Feminist Press, c1982.

D'emilio, John. *Making Trouble: Essays on Gay History, Politics, and the University.* New York: Routledge, 1992.

Dahl, Judy. *River of Promise: Two Women's Story of Love and Adoption.* San Diego: Lura Media, 1989.

Davies, Bob. *Mainstreamed Homosexuality: How the Rising Tide of Gay and Lesbian Activity is Affecting Church Ministry.* Leadership 16, p. 49-50, Article Libraries 276, 1995.

Dayringer, Richard. *Dealing with Depression: Five Pastoral Interventions.* New York: Haworth Pastoral Press, 1995.

Dayringer, Richard. *Homosexuality Reconsidered*: (scriptural, patristic, psychological and current theological perspectives: reply, L.

Graham, pp 97-104. Journal of Pastoral Care 50. Libraries: 489, 1996, p. 57-71.

Dean, Amy E. *Proud To Be*. New York: Bantum Books, 1994.

Dew, Robb Forman. *The Family Heart: A Memoir of When Our Son Came Out*. New York: Addison-Wesley, 1994.

Dicks, Russell, L. *Principles and Practices of Pastoral Care*. Philadelphia: Fortress Press, 1963.

_____. *Don't Lie to Homosexuals*. Christianity Today 37, p. 17. Article: Libraries 2851 1993.

Edwards, George R. *Gay/Lesbian Liberation: A Biblical Perspective*. New York: Pilgrim Press, 1984.

Egge, Doris Cline. *Homosexuality – The Congregations' Ministry*. Brethren Life and Thought 36, p. 9-51. Article: Libraries 129, 1991.

Ellison, Marvin. *Erotic Justice: A Liberating Ethic of Sexuality*. Kentucky: Westminster John Knox Press, 1996.

Faderman, Lillian. *Surpassing the Love of Men: Romantic Friendship and Love Between Women From the Renaissance to The Present*. New York: William Morrow, 1981.

Falco, Kristine L. *Psychotherapy with Lesbian Clients: Theory in Practice*. New York: Brunner/Mazel, 1991.

Fink, H.K. *They Stand Apart* (Review). Journal of Pastoral Care 11, p. 44-46. Libraries: 489, 1957.

Fischer, Kathleen. *Transforming Fire: Women Using Anger Creatively*. New York: Paulist Press, 1999.

Fortunato, John. *Embracing the Exile: Healing Journeys of Gay Christians*. Minneapolis: Winston-Seabury Press, 1983.

Fowler, James W. *Faith Development and Pastoral Care*. Philadelphia: Fortress Press, 1987.

Frye, Marilyn. "Lesbian 'Sex'." In *An Intimate Wilderness: Lesbian Writers on Sexuality*. ed. Judith Barrington. Oregon: The Eighth Mountain Press, 1991.

Furey, Pat, Jeannine Gramick. *The Vatican and Homosexuality: Reactions to the "Letter to the Bishops of the Catholic Church on the Pastoral Care of Homosexual Persons"*. New York: Crossroad, 1988.

Gaede, Beth Ann. *Congregations Talking About Homosexuality: Dialogue On A Difficult Issue*. Bethesda, Md.: Alban Institute, c1998.

Gaiser, Frederick J. *Sexual Orientation*: (Homosexuality in Lutheran context). Word and World 14. p 231-341. Libraries 173, 1994.

Gaiser, Frederick J. *"A New Word on Homosexuality?* Isiah 56:1-8 as Case Study." Word and World 14 (Sum 1994): 280-293.

Gennip, P A van. *Pastoral Care and Homosexual Persons: Whose Definitions?* New York: Crossroad, 1988.

Gerkin, Charles V. *Crisis in Modern Life: Theory & Theology for Pastoral Care*. Nashville: Abington, 1979.

Gerkin, Charles V. *The Living Human Document: Revisioning Pastoral Counseling in a Hermeneutical Mode*. Nashville:Abington Press, 1984.

Glaser, Chris. *Coming Out as Sacrament*. Kentucky: Westminster John Knox Press, 1998.

Goldberg, Martin. *Homosexuality*: (Review). Journal of Pastoral Care 23, p. 44-46: Libraries: 489, 1969.

Goodman, Bernice. "Lesbian Mothers." In *Keys to Caring: Assisting Your Gay and Lesbian Clients*, edited by Robert J. Jus, 119-24. Boston: Alyson, 1990.

Gordis, Robert. "Homosexuality and Traditional Religion." *Judaism* 32, No. 4 (Fall 1983): 405-9.

Graham, Larry Kent. *Care of Persons, Care of Worlds: A Psychosystems Approach to pastoral Care and Counseling.* Nashville, Abingdon Press, c1992.

Graham, Larry Kent. *How Should the Church Minister to Homosexual Persons and Their Families* (bibliog. study guide, pp 164-165). Caught in the Crossfire. P.157-165. Nashville: Abingdon Pr., 1994.

Graham, Larry Kent. *Discovering Images of God: Narratives of Care Among Lesbians and Gays.* Kentucky: Westminster John Knox Press, 1997.

Gramick, Jeannine and Pat Furey. *The Vatican and Homosexulaity: Reactions to the "Letter to the Bishops of the Catholic Church on the Pastoral Care of Homosexual Persons."* New York: Crossroad Publishing Company, 1988.

Greenberg, David, and Marcia H. Bystryn. "Christian Intolerance of Homosexuality." *American Journal of Sociology 88*, No. 3 (1982): 515-48.

Greene, Beverly. "Lesbian Women of Color: Triple Jeopardy." In *Women of Color: Integrating Ethnic and Gender Identities in Psychotherapy*, edited by Lillian Comas-Diaz and Beverly Greene, 389-427. New York: Guilford Press, 1994.

Griffin, Horace L. *Giving New Birth: Lesbians, Gays, and "The Family": A Pastoral Care Perspective* (bibliog.). Journal of Pastoral Theology 3: Libraries 84, 1993, p. 88-98.

Griffin, Horace L. "Revisioning Christian Ethical Discourse on Homosexuality: A Challenge for Pastoral Care in the 21st Century." AST Libraries: 495. *Journal of Pastoral Care 53*, 1999, pp. 209-219.

Groves, P. *Coming Out: Issues for the Therapist Working with Women in the Process of Lesbian Identity Formation.* Women & Therapy 4, 2 (Summer): 17-22, 1985.

Gutierres, Gustavo. *A Theology of Liberation*, trans. Sr. Caridad Inda and John Eagleson. New York: Orbis Books, 1973. (208)

Haeberle, Steen H. *The Role of Religious Organizations in the Gay and Lesbian Rights Movement.* Role of Religious Organizations in Social Movements, p. 71-89. New York: Praeger, 1991.

Hallet, Martin. *Sexual Identity and Freedom in Discipleship.* Cambridge: Grove Books Ltd, 1997.

Hasbany, Richard, ed. *Homosexuality and Religion.* New York: Harrington Park Press, 1989.

Harvey, Jane Hull. *Struggle for Recognition of Personal Worth.* (General Conference commends materials on homosexuality for church study). Christian Social Action 5, p. 9-11. Article: Libraries 239, 1992.

Hawley, John C. *A Challenge to Love* (book review). Libraries: 3034, 1983.

Heron, Ann (editor). *One Teenager in Ten: Writings by Gay and Lesbian Youth.* Boston: Alyson Publications, 1983.

Herzog, William R. *Parables As Subversive Speech: Jesus As Pedagogue Of The Oppressed.* Louisville, Kentucky: Westminster J. Knox Press, 1994.

Heyward, Carter. *Our Passion for Justice: Images of Power, Sexuality, and Liberation.* Ohio: Pilgrim Press, 1984.

Heyward, C. *The Redemption of God: A Theology of Mutual Relation.* Lanham, Md.: University Press of America, 1982.

Heyward, Carter. *Our Passion for Justice: Images of Power, Sexuality and Liberation*. New York: Pilgrim Press, 1984.

Heyward, Carter. *"Heterosexist Theology: Being Above It All."* Journal of Feminist Studies in Religion 3 (Spring): 29-38, 1987.

Heyward, Carter. *Speaking of Christ: A Lesbian Feminist Voice*. New York: Pilgrim Press, 1989.

Heyward, Carter. *Touching Our Strength: The Erotic as Power and the Love of God*. San Francisco: Harper Colllins Publishers, 1989.

Heyward, Carter. *Staying Power: Reflections on Gender, Justice and Compassion*. Ohio: The Pilgrim Press, 1995.

Hill, Anita C., Leo Treadway. *Rituals of Healing: Ministry With and On Behalf of Gay and Lesbian People*. Lift Every Voice, p. 231-244. San Francisco: Harper & Row, 1990.

Hoagland, Sara. *Lesbian Ethics: Toward New Value*. Palo Alto, Cal.: Institute of Lesbian Studies, 1988.

Hochstein, L. *Pastoral Counselors: Their Attitudes Toward Gay and Lesbian Clients*. Journal of Pastoral Care 40, 2 (June): 158-63, 1986.

Holtz, Raymond C. *Listen To The Stories: Gay and Lesbian Catholics Talk About Their Lives and The Church*. New York: Garland, 1991.

Hunt, M. *On Religious Lesbians: Contradictions and Challenges*. in D. Altman, et al., *Homosexuality, Which Homosexuality?* (pp. 97-113), 1989.

Ip, King-Tak. *Homosexuality and the Church*. Hill Road 2, No. 2, 1999, p. 9-149.

Jackson, Edgar N. *Understanding Grief, It's Roots, Dynamics, and Treatment*. Nashville: Abingdon Press, 1957.

Jackson, Edgar N. *The Many Faces of Grief.* Nashville: Abington Press, 1977.

Kaufman, Gershen and Lev Raphael. *Coming Out of Shame: Transforming Gay and Lesbian Lives.* New York: Doubleday, 1996.

Johnson, A.E. *Homosexuality and Counseling*: (Review). Journal of Pastoral Care 31, p. 67-68, Libraries: 489, 1977.

Kosnik, A. and W. Carroll, A. Cunningham, R. Modras, J. Schulte. *Human Sexuality: New Directions in American Thought.* New York: Paulist Press, 1977.

Kübler-Ross, Elizabeth. *On Death and Dying.* New York: Macmillan Publishing Co., 1969.

Laird, Joan, Green, Robert-Jay (editors), McGoldrick, Monica (foreword). *Lesbians and Gays in Couples and Families: A Handbook for Therapists.* San Francisco: Jossey-Bass Publishers, c1996.

Lebacqz, Karen. *Appropriate Vulnerability. In Sexuality and the Sacred: Sources for Theological Reflection,* eds. James Nelson and Sandra Longfellow. Kentucky: Westminster John Knox Press, 1994.

Leopold, Kathleen, Thomas Orians. *Theological Pastoral Resources: A Collection of Articles on Homosexuality from a Pastoral Perspective.* Washington, DC: Dignity, 1981.

Legge, Marilyn. *The Grace of Difference: A Canadian Feminist Theological Ethic.* Atlanta: Scholars Press, 1992.

Leopold, Kathleen and Thomas Orians. Theological Pastoral Resources: A Collection of Articles on Homosexuality from a Pastoral Perspective, 6th ed. Washington, DC: Dignity, 1981.

Linscheid, John. "Creating Companionship: The God of Genesis Call Us All – Gay and Straight – from Loneliness to Relationship." Other Side 31 (S-01995):8-11, 14-15.

Linscheid, John. "Our Story in God's Story: Reading the Bible with Gay Eyes." *Other Side* 23 (Jl-Ag 1987): 32-35+.

Lorde, Audre. *Sister Outsider.* Freedom, California: Crossing Press, 1984.

Lum, doman. *Responding to Suicidal Crisis: For Church and Community.* Grand Rapids: Eerdmans, 1974.

Markowitz, Laura M. "When Same-Sex Couples Divorce." *Family Therapy Networker 18*, No. 3 (May/June 1994): 31-33.

Marshall, Joretta L. *Counseling Lesbian Partners* (Counseling and Pastoral Theology). Louisville: Westminster John Knox Press, 1997.

McCann, Richard Vincent. *The Churches and Mental Health.* New York: Basic Books, 1962.

McNeill, John J. Freedom, *Glorious Freedom: The Spiritual Journey to the Fullness of Life for Gays, Lesbians, and Everybody Else.* Boston: Beacon Press, 1995.

McNeill, John J. *The Church and the Homosexual.* Kansas City, Kansas: Sheed Andrews and McMeel, C1976.

McNeill, John J. *The Church and The Homosexual.* Boston: Beacon Press, 1976.

McNeill, John J. *Taking a Chance on God: Liberating Theology for Gays, Lesbians, and Their Lovers, Families, and Friends.* Boston, Mass.: Beacon Press, 1988.

McNeill, John J. *Tapping Deeper Roots: Integrating the Spiritual Dimension into Professional Practice with Lesbian and Gay Clients.* Journal of Pastoral Care 48. Libraries: 489, 1994, p. 313-324.

Miller, Isabel. *Patience and Sarah.* New York: McGraw-Hill, 1972.

Miller, J.B. *Toward a New Psychology of Women*, 2d ed. Boston: Beacon, 1986.

Moberly, Elizabeth R. *First Aid in Pastoral Care, 15: Counselling the Homosexual*. Expository Times 96. Libraries: 437, 1985, p. 261-266.

Mollenkott, Virginia Ramey. *Omnigender: A Trans-religious Approach*. Ohio: Pilgrim Press, 2001.

Monourquette, John. *How To Befriend Your Shadow: Welcoming Your Unloved Side*. Ottawa: Novalis, 2001.

Morse, Janice, ed. "Emerging From the Data: The Cognitive Processes of Analysis in Qualitative Inquiry". *In Critical Issues in Qualitative Research Methods*. California: Sage Publications, 1994.

Morrison, Melanie. *The Grace of Coming Home: Spirituality, Sexuality, and the Struggle for Justice*. Cleveland: Pilgrim Press, 1995.

Murchison, D. Cameron, Jr. "An Awful Rowing Toward God: A Review of Some recent Literature from the Church's Conversation on Homosexuality." (Critic's Corner). *Theology Today* 53 (Ja 1997) p. 508-513, Article Libraries 939.

_____. and Murphy, B. *Therapeutic Work with Lesbian Clients: A Systemic Therapy View*. In *Women and Family Therapy*, edited by Marianne Ault-Riche, pp. 78-89. Rockville, Md.: Aspen Systems Corporation, 1986.

Murray, Elwood J. "A Search for God in Story and Time." *America 169*, No. 11 (October 16, 1993): 10-13.

Neff, David. *The New Ex-gay Agenda*. (homosexual ministries; editorial). Christianity Today 36, p. 21. Article: Libraries 2851, 1992.

Nelson, James B. *Between Two Gardens: Reflections on Sexuality and Religious Experience*. New York: The Pilgrim Press, 1983.

Nelson, James B. *Body Theology*. Louisville: Westminster John Knox Press, 1992.

Nelson, James and Sandra Longfellow, eds. *Sexuality and the Sacred: Sources for Theological Reflection*. Kentucky: Westminster John Knox Press, 1994.

Neuger, Christie Cozad, editor. *The Arts of Ministry: Feminist-womanist Approaches*. Louisville, Kentucky: Westminster John Knox Press, c1996.

Neuger, Christie Cozad. *Counseling Women: A Narrative, Pastoral Approach*. Minneapolis, Minnesota: Fortress Press, c2001.

Newbigin, Leslie. *The Good Shepherd*. Leighton Buzzard, Beds: The Faith Press, 1977.

Nicoloff, L., and E. Stiglitz. *Lesbian Alcoholism: Etiology Treatment and Recovery*. In *Boston Lesbian Psychologies Collective, Lesbian Psychologies*, (pp. 283-93). 1987.

Nouwen, Henri. *The Wounded Healer*. New York: Doubleday, 1972.

Nouwen, Henri, J. *Lifesigns: Intimacy, Fecundity, Ecstasy in Christian Perspective*. New York: Doubleday, 1986.

Nova Scotia Advisory Council on the Status of Women. "Letting In A Little Light: Lesbians and Their Families in Nova Scotia." Nova Scotia Department of Supply and Services, Publishing Section, 1996.

Nugent, Robert. *Married Homosexuals*. Journal of Pastoral Care 37. Libraries: 489, p. 243-251, 1983.

Nugent, Robert and Jeannine Gramick. *Building Bridges: Gay and Lesbian Reality and the Catholic Church*. Mystic, Connecticut: Twenty-third Publications, 1992.

O'Neill, Craig and Kathleen Ritter, *Coming Out Within: Stages of Spiritual Awakening for Lesbians and Gay Men*. San Francisco: Harper Collins Publishers, 1992.

Oden, Thomas C. *Recovering Lost Identity*. Journal of Pastoral Care 34, no. 1, 1980.

Oates, Thomas C.. *Pastoral Theology: Essentials of Ministry*. Harper & Row, 1982.

Oden, Thomas C. (Browning, Don S, editor). *Care of Souls in the Classic Tradition*. Philadelphia: Fortress Press, c1984.

Oates, Wayne E. *The Bible and Pastoral Care*. Grand Rapids, Michigan, 1952.

Oates, Wayne E. *Christ and Selfhood*. New York: Association Press, 1961.

Oates, Wayne E. *Pastoral Care and Counseling in Grief and Separation*. Philadephia: Fortress Press, 1970.

Oates, Wayne E. *New Dimensions In Pastoral Care*. Philadelphia: Fortress Press, 1970.

Oates, Wayne Edward. *Pastoral Counseling*. Philadelphia: Westminster Press, 1974.

Oates, Wayne E. *Grief, Transition and Loss*: A Pastor's Practical Guide. Minneapolis: Fortress Press, 1997.

Oglesby, William B. *Biblical Themes for Pastoral Care*. Nashville: Abingdon, c1980.

Oglesby, William B. *Biblical Themes for Pastoral Care*. Nashville: Abingdon, 1983.

Padesky, C. *Attaining and Maintaining Positive Lesbian Self-Identify: A Cognitive Therapy Approach.* Women & Therapy 8, 1-2: 145-56, 1988.

Pantaleo, Jack. *The Opened Tomb.* (meaning of Lazarus story for homosexual Christians). Other Side 28, p. 8-12. Article: Libraries 304, 1992.

Parker, Simon B. "*The Hebrew Bible and Homosexuality: (Hospitality, Law, Taboo in Ancient Israel;* bibliog..)" Quarterly Review 11 (Fall 1991): 4-19.

Parkes, Colin Murray. *Bereavement: Studies of Grief In Adult Life.* New York: International Press, 1972.

Parsons, Richard D. and Robert J. Wicks, editors. Clinical Handbook of Pastoral Counseling, Volume 2, p 229. New York: Paulist Press, 1993.

Pekich, Barbara. *Communion of the Saints: (unchurched) Homosexuals Discover God's Grace in Lord's Supper*; opinion. Perspectives 12, p. 6, Article Libraries: 227, 1997.

Pellegrin, W.B.H. *To Live According To Our Nature: The Gay Presence In The Anglican Church of Canada.* Newport, NS, c1993.

Perry, Troy D. *Don't Be Afraid Anymore: The Story of Reverend Troy Perry and the Metropolitan Community Churches.* New York: St. Martin's Press, 1990.

Pierson, Lance. *No-gay Areas: Pastoral Care of Homosexual Christians.* Bramcote, England: Grove Books, 1989.

Quinn, John R. *Toward An Understanding of the Letter* "On the pastoral care of homosexual persons." (repr; replay, W. Shannon, pp 20-27). New York: Crossroad, 1988.

Rafkin, Louise. *Different Mothers: Sons and Daughters of Lesbians Talk About Their Lives*. Pittsburgh: Cleis Press, 1990.

Ratliff, J. Bill (editor). *Out of the Silence: Quaker Perspectives on Pastoral Care and Counseling*. Wallingford, PA: Pendle Hill Pub. c2001.

Ratzinger, Joseph, Cardinal. *Letters to the Bishops of the Catholic Church on the Pastoral Care of Homosexual Persons* (1986). Louisville, Ky: Westminster/John Knox Pr., 1994.

Raymond, Janice G. *A Passion For Friends: Toward a Philosophy of Female Affection*. Boston: Beacon Press, 1986.

Ready or Not, Queer We Come. Address given at Queer Justice/Queer Holiness Conference, Church of Holy Trinity, Toronto, Canada, December 9, 2000.

Reiter, Laura. *Sexual Orientation, Sexual Identity, and the Question of Choice*. Clinical Social Work Journal 17, 2 (Summer): 138-50, 1989.

Rich, Adrienne Ceclie. *On Lies Secrets, and Silence: Selected Prose*. New York: W.W. Norton and Company, 1979.

Rich, Adrienne. "Compulsory Heterosexuality and Lesbian Existence", In *Signs*, 1980 (Vol. 5, No. 4), p 631-660.

Rigali, Norbert J. The Vatican and Homosexuality. Horizons 16. Libraries: 272, p. 191-192, 1989.

Riordon, Michael. *The First Stone: Homosexuality and The United Church*. Toronto: McClelland & Stewart, c1990.

Ritter, Kathleen and Craig O'Neill. "Moving Through Loss: The Spiritual Journey of Gay Men and Lesbian Women." *Journal of Counseling and Development* 68. September/October 1989: 9-15.

Roberts, Stan. *Pastoring the Far Side: Making a Place for Believing Homoseuals* (Interview by Elbert Peck; repr fr F 1990; ils). Libraries: 43 (ATLAReligion): Sunstone 22 (Je 1999), p 88-97.

Robinson, N.H.G. *Christ and Conscience.* London: Nisbet, 1956.

Rogers, C. *On Becoming a Person.* Boston: Houghton Mifflin, 1961.

Roth, S. *Psychotherapy with Lesbian Couples: Individual Issues, Female Socialization and the Social Context.* In M. McGoldrick et al., *Women in Families.* New York: W.W. Norton. 1989.

Savin-Williams, Ritch and Kenneth M. Cohen. *The Lives of Lesbians, Gays, and Bisexuals: Children to Adults.* New York: Harcourt Brace and Company, 1996.

Scanzoni, Letha, and Virginia Ramey Mollenkott. *Is the Homosexual My Neighbor? Another Christian View.* New York: Harper & Row, 1980.

Scroggs, R. *The New Testament and Homosexuality.* Philadelphia: Fortress Press, 1983.

Seow, Choon-Leong, ed. *Homosexuality and Christian Community.* Louisville: Westminster John Knox Press, 1996.

Shallenberger, David. *Gifts of Gay and Lesbian Ministry.* Pastoral Psychology 43, p. 105-113. Article: Libraries 525, 1994.

Shallenberger, David. *The Exodus and Spiritual Odyssey of Gays and Lesbian.* Religious Humanism 28, p. 139-143. Article: Libraries 309, 1994.

Shannon, William H. *A Response to Archbishop Quinn*: ("Toward an understanding of the letter 'On the pastoral care of homosexual persons'.") pp 13-19. New York: Crossroad, 1988.

Shapiro, David Sidney. *The Mental Health Counselor in the Community, Training of Physicians and Ministers.* Springfield, Ill.:C.C. Thomas, 1968.

Sheppard, Gerald T. "The Use of Scriptures Within the Christian Ethical Debate Concerning Same-sex Oriented Persons." *Union Seminary Quarterly Review* 40 No 1-2(1985):13-35.

Siker, Jeffrey S., ed. *Homosexuality in the Church: Both Sides of the Debate*. Louisville: Westminster John Knox Press, 1994.

Sinfield, Alan. *Out On Stage: Lesbian and Gay Theatre in the Twentieth Century*. New Haven, Ct.: Yale University Press, 1999.

Slater, Suzanne. *Lesbian Family Life Cycle*. New York: Free Press, 1995.

Soards, Marion L. *Scripture and Homosexuality: Biblical Authority and the Church Today*. Louisville, Kentucky: Westminster John Knox Press, 1995.

Smith, Leon. *Theological, Ethical and Pastoral Care Perspectives*. Nashville: Discipleship Resources, 1981.

Southard, Samuel. *Training Church Members for Pastoral Care*. Valley Forge, PA: Judson Press, 1982.

Stone, Howard W. *The Caring Church: A Guide for Lay Pastoral Care*. San Francisco: Harper & Row, c1983.

Stone, Howard W. *The Word of God and Pastoral Care*. Nashville: Abingdon Press, c1988.

Stone, Kenneth Alan. "Gender and Homosexuality in Judges 19: Subject – Honor, Object-Shame? *Journal for the Study of the Old Testament* 67 (S1995): 87-107.

Strieter, Thomas W. *Theological Reflections on Pastoral Care for Gay (sic) and Lesbians*: (fr. Lutheran and Scriptural Viewpoint). Currents in Theology and Mission 20. Libraries: 171, 1993, p 268-277.

Strunk, Orio, Jr. ed. *Symposium on Homosexuality and Pastoral Counseling*. Journal of Pastoral Care 50 (Spr 1996), p. 57-104. Article Libraries 495.

Stuart, Elizabeth. "Lesbian and Gay Spirituality: A Lesbian Feminist Perspective." In *Christian Perspectives on Sexuality and Gender*, eds. Adrian Thatcher and Elizabeth Stuart. Michigan: Eerdmans Publishing Company, 1996.

Stuart, Elizabeth and Andy Braunston, Malcolm Edwards, John McMahon, Tim Morrison. *Religion is A Queer Thing: A Guide to the Christian Faith for Lesbian, Gay, Bisexual and Transgendered People*. Ohio: The Pilgrim Press, 1997.

Switzer, David K. *The Dynamics of Grief.* Nashville: Abingdon Press, c1970.

Switzer, David K. *The Minister as Crisis Counselor*. Nashville: Abingdon Press, 1974.

Switzer, David K. (Switzer, Shirley). *Parents of the Homosexual*. Philadelphia, Pennsylvania: Westminster Press, c1980.

Switzer, David K. *Pastoral Care and Homosexuality*. Nashville: Discipleship Resources, 1981.

Switzer, David K. *Now Who's Coming to Dinner? Pastoral Care for Family and Friends of Gay and Lesbian People*. Word & World 14. Libraries 173, 1994.

Switzer, David K. *Coming Out as Parents: You and Your Homosexual Child*. Louisville, Kentucky: Westminster John Knox Press, c1996.

Switzer, David K., John Thornburg (concluding chapter). *Pastoral Care of Gays, Lesbians, and Their Families*. Minneapolis, Minnesota: Fortress Press, c1999.

Tam, Ekman P.C. *Ethical Issues in Counseling with Gay and Lesbian Clients: Coversion Therapy and Confidentiality Limits*. Journal of Pastoral Care 51. Libraries: 489, 1997, p. 13-24

Tanner, Donna M. *The Lesbian Couple.* Lexington, MA: D.C. Heath & Co., 1978.

Thistlethwaite, Susan Brooks and Mary Potter Engel, eds. *Lift Every Voice: Constructing Christian Theologies from the Underside.* New York: Harper and Row, 1990.

Thorne, Brian. *Person-Centred Counselling and Christian Spirituality: The Secular and The Holy.* London: Whurr, 1998.

Tigert, Leanne McCall, *Coming Out While Staying In: Struggles and Celebrations of Lesbians, Gays, and Bisexuals in the Church.* Cleveland, Ohio: United Church Press, 1996.

Tigert, Leanne McCall. *Coming Out Through Fire: Surviving the Trauma of Homophobia.* Ohio: United Church Press, 1999.

Topper, C. *Spirituality as a Component in Counseling Lesbians-Gays. The Journal of Pastoral Counseling* 21, 1- (Spring-Summer): 55-59, 1986.

Tournier, Paul. *Guilt and Grace: A Psychological Study.* San Francisco: Harper and Row, 1962.

Trible, Phyllis. *Texts of Terror.* Philadelphia: Fortress Press, 1984.

Trumbach, Randolph. "The Origin and Development of the Modern Lesbian Role in the Western Gender System: Northwestern Europe and the United States." 1750-1990 Lesbian Histories; Review Essay. *Historical Reflections* 20 (Sum 1994), p. 287-320: Article Libraries: 174.

Unrepentant, Self-Affirming, Practising: Lesbian, Bisexual, Gay. New York: Continuum, 1996.

Unterberger, Gail. *Counseling Lesbians: A Feminist Perspective* (bibliog.). Clinical Handbook of Pastoral Counseling, vol. 2. p. 228-266 (essay). New York: Paulist, 1993.

_____ed. *Voices of Hope: A Collection of Positive Catholic Writings on Gay and Lesbian Issues.* Maryland: New Ways Ministry, 1995.

Walker, Alice. *The Colour Purple.* New York: Harcourt Brace Jovanovich, 1982.

Wat, Benjamin. *Pastoral Care for the Homosexuals: (Eng abst, p124).* ATLA Religion: Hill Road 2, no 2 (1999), p. 124-149.

Weegraff, John. The Vatican and Homosexuality (Review). Journal of Ecumenical Studies 26. Libraries: 746, p. 555-556, 1989.

Wenham, Gordon J. "The Old Testament Attitude to Homosexuality." *Expository Times* 102 (S 1991): 359-363.

Weston, Kath. *Families We Choose: Lesbians, Gays, Kinship.* New York: Columbia University Press, 1991.

White, William R. *Stories for Telling.* Minneapolis: Augsburg Publishing House, 1986.

Williams, Bruce. *The Vatican and Homosexuality*: (Review). Thomist 54, Libraries: 490, p. 160-164, 1990.

Williams Daniel Day. *The Minister and the Care of Souls.* New York: Harper & Row, c1961.

Williams Daniel Day. *The Spirit and the Forms of Love.* New York: Harper & Row, 1968.

Wilson, Earl D. *Counseling and Homosexuality.* Waco, Tex.: Word Books, 1988.

Winnicott, D.W. *The Maturational Process and the Facilitating Environment: Studies in the Theory of Emotional Development.* New York: International Universities Press, 1965.

Wise, Carroll A. *The Meaning of Pastoral Care*. New York: Harper & Bros., 1966.

Wolf, Susan J., Stanley, Julia Penelope (editors). *The Coming Out Stories*. Watertown, Massachusetts: Persephone Press, c1980.

Woods, Richard. *Another Kind of Love: Homosexuality and Spirituality*. Ft. Wayne, IN: Knoll Pub. Co., 1988.

Zanottie, B., ed. *A Faith of One's Own: Explorations by Catholic Lesbians*. Trumansburg, New York: Crossing Press.

www.ingramcontent.com/pod-product-compliance
Lightning Source LLC
LaVergne TN
LVHW041841070526
838199LV00045BA/1388